My First Cardigan Workbook™

Georgia Druen

Annie's™

This book is designed to be used as a self-guided tutorial or as the workbook for a class at a local yarn shop.

The small size of the baby sweater will let you pack the most learning into a compact project with the least amount of plain knitting. At the end of each section, you'll have a wonderful gift to give immediately or store away for a future arrival.

Work through the sweaters in the order presented, or make the basic pattern and jump straight to the technique you most desire.

When you've completed the baby-sized options, progress to a sweater for yourself. Impatient with the baby option? Feel free to jump right into an adult size. The techniques are the same, and the pattern is ready to go!

With over 20 years of experience as a knitting instructor, designer and owner of HearthStone Knits, a local yarn shop in St. Louis, Mo., I have guided hundreds of knitters through their first sweater. Let me guide you through the wonderful world of cardigan sweaters.

Happy knitting!

Georgia

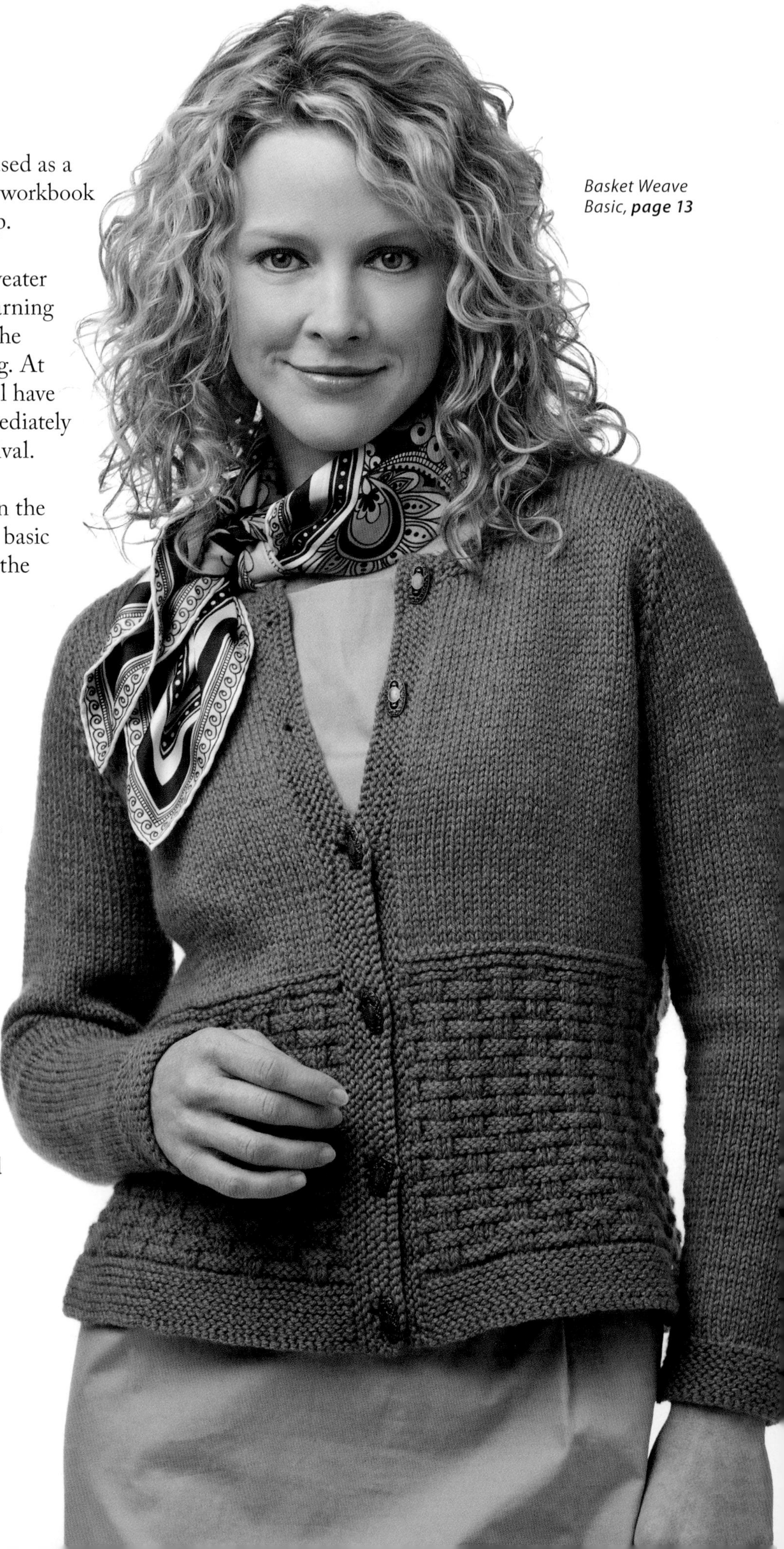

Basket Weave Basic, ***page 13***

Table of Contents

Baby Blocks, ***page 7***

Diamonds & Lace, ***page 42***

Annie's™ *My First Cardigan Workbook* is published by Annie's, 306 East Parr Road, Berne, IN 46711. Printed in USA.

Every effort has been made to ensure that the instructions in this pattern book are complete and accurate. We cannot, however, take responsibility for human error, typographical mistakes or variations in individual work. Please visit AnniesCustomerCare.com to check for pattern updates.

ISBN: 978-1-59635-625-2

1 2 3 4 5 6 7 8 9

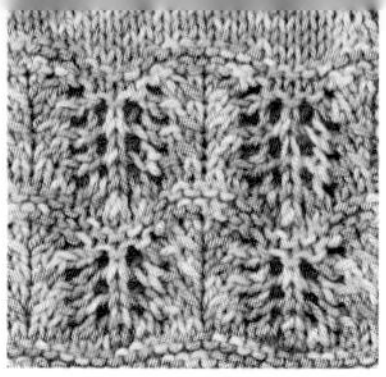

Before You Get Started

These are the basic necessities of sweater knitting, so get comfortable and read through this section before you proceed with your first cardigan.

Materials

The yarns used in the models are widely available, but if your local yarn shop does not carry the one you need, the staff should be able to guide you to an appropriate alternative. If you're choosing the substitute on your own, there are some basic rules to follow.

Labels are your friends! Read carefully to determine not only the classification (CYC #4 Medium) of the yarn, but also the recommended stitch gauge. If the label suggests 16 stitches per 4 inches and your pattern requires 20 stitches per 4 inches (both in category #4), move on to another yarn.

Choose quantity based on yardage, not on weight. Various fibers will yield a different number of yards per ounce, and the yardage determines how many stitches you can get out of a skein.

Choosing Your Size

Please, please, please don't choose your sweater size based on bra size! Bra sizes are measured in a completely different way.

Grab a tape measure and a find a buddy. Swear her to silence and have her measure the fullest part of your bust. Add about 3 inches for ease if you plan to wear the sweater over another garment. That is your size.

No buddy available? Find your favorite cardigan of similar weight and lay it out flat on a smooth surface. Measure across the body at the underarm; double that number. This is your preferred finished size.

All of the adult sweaters except the Adult Lace are designed in unisex sizing. Be sure to check the sweater measurements against your own sleeve and body length before beginning.

Making Adjustments

If you adjust sleeve length, remember to redistribute the spacing of the decreases. The adult sweaters have options for custom sleeve lengths.

Remember to recalculate the buttonhole spacing if you change the body length. The basic rules of buttonhole placement call for the top button to be approximately ½ inch from the top (more if a larger button is used) and the bottom button at the midpoint of the bottom border (but no less than ½ inch from the bottom edge). The remaining buttons are evenly spaced between these two.

Long or short waisted? The instructions for the optional waist shaping have built-in adjustments.

Gauge

So many knitters brag that they never do a tension swatch. I'm always tempted to ask them how many of their projects fit the way they want. We refer to knitting garments without doing gauge swatches as "The Texas Gambler Method." Please don't be tempted to skip, skimp or lie to yourself about this step.

If there are multiple stitch patterns in your project, bite the bullet and work a gauge swatch for all of them. You may need to change needle sizes for the pattern stitch, especially when changing between one- and two-color stockinette stitch.

For these sweaters, as for most sweaters, stitch gauge is the critical issue. Row gauge is less important.

Architecture

Right front, left front? Top down? Where am I? This photo will help you anchor yourself.

The left/right designations are as the sweater will be worn—not as they appear on the needle.

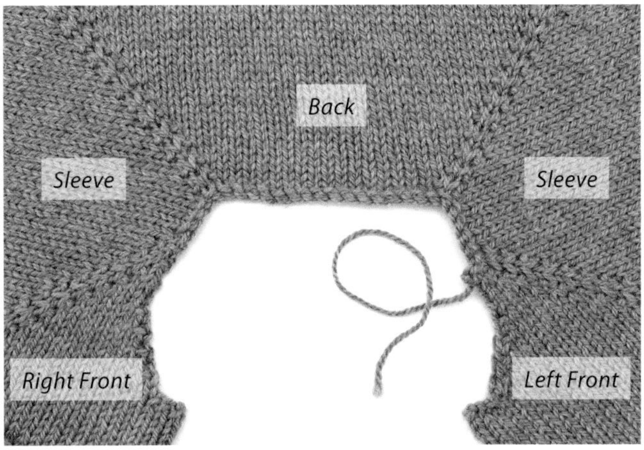

Keeping Track

Measure your work from the designated point to immediately under the needle. Do not include the needle or its cable in the measurement.

Inserting a boundary line is an excellent way to create a point from which to measure. These patterns call for inserting one on each sleeve in the underarm cast-on row. (For other projects I always add them in the same row as the underarm bind-off for ease in measuring the depth of an armhole.) To insert a boundary line, you will need a 5-inch strand of smooth, lightweight yarn in a contrasting color. Work a few stitches into the row you will mark, then lay the strand between the point of your needles with the longest portion to the front of the work. It will rest directly on top of your work. Work two stitches. Flip the long end between the points of the needles so it lays to the back of the work. Work two stitches and flip it forward. Repeat a couple more times until you have a dotted line of yarn on the right side.

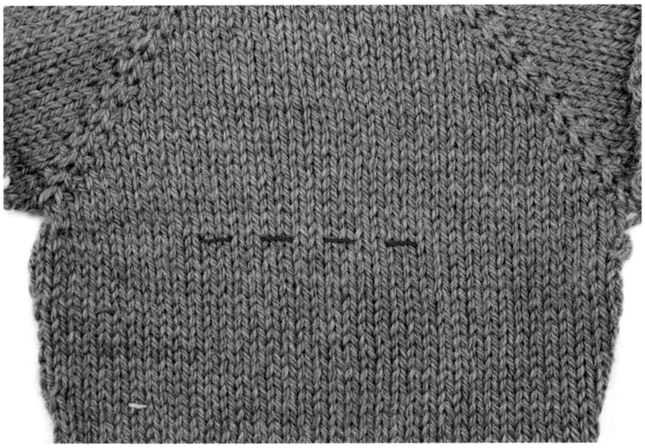

Red boundary line at underarm cast-on row. Pink marker on decrease rows.

Instructions for the spacing of sleeve decreases can be given by row count or by measurement. The row-count method requires careful adherence to row gauge and accurate counting, while the use of measurements requires the marking of each shaping row and accurate measuring. These patterns use the measurement option. Be sure to mark every decrease row in the sleeve with either a removable marker or a boundary line (use a different color than you used at the underarm to avoid confusion). This mark should be placed in the decrease row as you are working it. It may not always be possible for the specified measurement to work out to be a right-side row. If you are one row too short in the space between two decreases, work one row longer between the next two decreases (and vice versa, of course). Whatever method you are using, periodically check the overall length of the sleeve and compare it to the number of decreases remaining to see whether it's necessary to change the spacing between decreases in order to achieve the proper sleeve length. Be sure to measure accurately because discrepancies of even fractions of an inch can mount up quickly.

Knitting Techniques

In order to cast on at the underarms and the front neck edges, it's necessary to use a knitted cast-on. There are several forms of this type of cast-on including knitting on and the cable cast-on (see page 63).

Three types of increases are used in this book: M1 (make one), kfb (knit in front and back of stitch), and yo (yarn over).

Mattress stitch (sometimes known as "vertical grafting") makes a beautiful seam. Since it is done with the right side facing, it is easy to line up the decreases on each side of the underarm seam.

"Pick up and knit" means exactly that. Insert

the point of the right needle into the fabric where you want the picked-up stitch to be, wrap the yarn around that needle and draw up the new stitch. Voilà! When picking up stitches along a vertical edge, it is important to follow the "trough" between the edge stitch and one next to it. That way the stitches will be picked up under two strands of yarn to prevent stretching out and they will follow a straight line.

Finishing Touches

Blocking

The issue of blocking raises questions—and fears. Once again, the yarn label is your friend. It will tell you the fiber content, washing instructions and sometimes the heat tolerance. The heat tolerance is indicated by the icon of the iron. The more dots under the iron, the more heat the fiber can tolerate.

If your label says "dry clean only," do not wet-block. If your fiber has much synthetic content, be wary of using too much heat. It will "kill" synthetics like acrylic and nylon. In this case "killing" the yarn means it has lost elasticity and body and has become limp and lifeless.

Wool will endure much in the way of heat and moisture unless combined with agitation—that way leads to felting.

What can you do safely? Pin out the garment, as per the above cautions, spritz with water—or steam lightly—and let dry in place. Do not rest the iron directly on the fabric.

Buttons

The adult model sweaters used 1-inch buttons, but buttons from ¾ up to 1 inch are acceptable alternatives.

I recommend backer buttons for all knitwear. They prevent the buttons from being pulled through the knitted fabric only to droop and dangle from the sweater front, a common hazard on children's garments. They also add stability to larger buttons. With prolonged use, sewing thread can cut through yarn, and backer buttons mitigate the thread's sawing effect on your stitches.

Now choose your pattern and let's begin! •

Baby Blocks

This sweater is so fast and easy you'll have it finished in no time—and learn a lot along the way. The pattern includes instructions for an optional texture pattern to add an extra kiss of style.

Skill level

Easy

Sizes

	6 mo	12 mo	18 mo	24 mo
Baby with standard fit				
Finished Measurements				
Chest (buttoned): inches	21	21¾	22¾	24
Length: inches	11¾	11¾	12¼	12¼
Materials				
Berroco Vintage DK (DK weight; 50% acrylic/ 40% wool/10% nylon; 288 yds/100g per hank): hanks fuchsia #21176 (shown on model) or cerulean #21190 (shown on swatch) (3 LIGHT)	2	2	3	3

- Size 6 (4mm) 32-inch circular needle or size needed to obtain gauge
- Stitch markers
- 5 (½-inch) buttons #12548 from JHB International
- 5 (½-inch) backer buttons #40800 from JHB International
- Piece of smooth, lightweight scrap yarn approx 5 inches long in a contrasting color
- Sewing thread to match sweater color

Gauge

22 sts and 28 rows = 4 inches/10cm in St st and Baby Bricks pat.
To save time, take time to check gauge.

Tip

Stitch gauge is critical; row gauge is less so.

Special Abbreviations

Make 1 (M1): Insert LH needle from front to back under the designated running thread between sts; knit into the back of resulting loop.

Double yarn over (2yo): Yo twice. On next row, work (k1, p1) into 2yo.

Slip marker (sm): Slip marker from LH to RH needle.

Pattern Stitch

***Note:** A chart is provided for those preferring to work pat st from a chart.*

Baby Bricks (multiple of 4 sts + 1)

Row 1 (RS): Knit.

Row 2: *K3, p1, rep from * to last st, k1.

Row 3: P1, *k1, p3, rep from * to end.

Row 4: Purl.

Row 5: *P3, k1, rep from * to last st, p1.

Row 6: K1, *p1, k3, rep from * to end.

Rep Rows 1–6 for pat.

Pattern Note

Before beginning, be sure to read the Before You Get Started section for complete information on top-down architecture, seaming techniques, size selection and more.

Yoke

Cast on ___ sts.	31	34	36	38
Set-up row (WS): P ___ right front sts, pm,	2	2	2	2
p ___ right sleeve sts, pm,	5	6	7	8
p ___ back sts, pm,	17	18	18	18
p ___ left sleeve sts, pm,	5	6	7	8
p ___ left front sts.	2	2	2	2
Row 1 (RS): [Knit to 1 st before marker, kfb, sm, kfb] 4 times, knit to end. ***Note:** Each completed Row 1 adds 8 sts.*				
___ sts	39	42	44	46

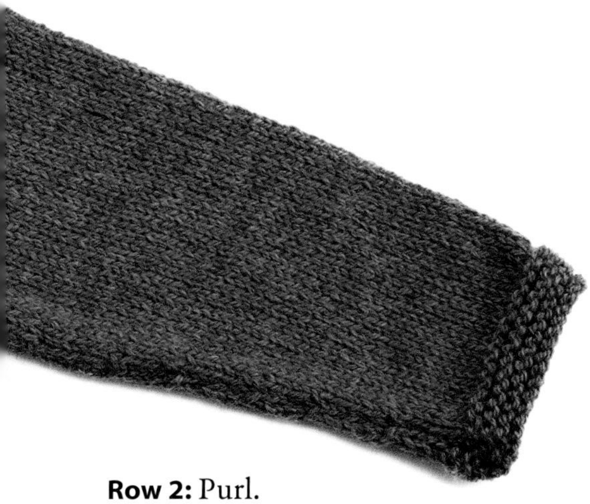

Tip

In order to cast on at the beg of a row, it is necessary to use a knitted cast-on.

Row 2: Purl.				
Rep [Rows 1 and 2] twice more.				
sts	**55**	**58**	**60**	**62**

Shape Front Neck Edge

Row 3 (RS): Kfb, [knit to 1 st before marker, kfb, sm, kfb] 4 times, knit to last 2 sts, kfb, k1. ***Note:** Each completed Row 3 adds 10 sts.*				
sts	**65**	**68**	**70**	**72**
Row 4: Purl.				
Rep Rows 3 and 4 times more.	**3**	**4**	**4**	**4**
sts	**95**	**108**	**110**	**112**
Next row (RS): Cast on 4 sts, [knit to 1 st before marker, kfb, sm, kfb] 4 times, knit to end.				
sts	**107**	**120**	**122**	**124**
Next row (WS): Cast on 4 sts, purl to end. The neck edge shaping is now complete.				
sts	**111**	**124**	**126**	**128**
Work Rows 1 and 2 times more.	**8**	**7**	**9**	**10**
Work 1 row even or until center back measures at least inches from cast-on edge, ending with a RS row.	**5**	**5**	**5½**	**5¾**
total sts	**175**	**180**	**198**	**208**
sts each front	**26**	**27**	**29**	**30**
sts each sleeve	**37**	**38**	**43**	**46**
back sts	**49**	**50**	**54**	**56**

Tip

Even though you did a tension swatch, now is the time to double check your gauge. Why? When you worked your swatch you were concentrating on tension; now that you're working on the sweater itself, your mind is on other aspects of your knitting. Gauge can reflect that difference. Measure your gauge at least ¾ inch below the needle across 4 inches on the sweater back. If gauge is different, bite the bullet and reknit after switching to the appropriate needle size.

Divide for Right Sleeve

With WS facing, purl across right front to first marker and right sleeve sts to 2nd marker; remove this marker and turn.

Right Sleeve

*Cast on 3 sts; knit to marker, adding a boundary line near center of sleeve; remove this marker and turn.

sleeve sts	**40**	**41**	**46**	**49**
Cast on 3 sts; purl across sleeve.				
sleeve sts	**43**	**44**	**49**	**52**
Work even until sleeve measures inch(es) from boundary line, ending with a WS row.	¾	1	1½	1¾
Dec row (RS): K1, k2tog, knit to last 3 sts, ssk, k1.				
sts	**41**	**42**	**47**	**50**
[Work ¾ inch even, ending with a WS row; work Dec row] 5 times.				
sts	**31**	**32**	**37**	**40**
Work even until sleeve measures inches from boundary line or ¾ inch less than desired length, ending with a WS row.	5¾	6¾	7¼	7¾
Dec row (RS): Knit and dec sts evenly spaced across row.	**3**	**3**	**4**	**4**
sts	**28**	**29**	**33**	**36**

Knit 6 rows.

Bind off loosely in knit on WS.

Cut yarn, leaving a long tail. Use this tail to sew sleeve seam using mattress st.

Divide for Left Sleeve

With WS facing, attach yarn to sweater back adjacent to base of completed right sleeve. Purl across back sts to first marker and left sleeve sts to 2nd marker; remove this marker and turn.

Left Sleeve

Complete as for right sleeve.

Body

With WS facing, attach yarn to front of sweater adjacent to base of completed left sleeve. Purl across left front sts.

Unification row (RS): Knit across left front sts; *M1 using loose strand between previous section and sleeve, pick up and knit 4 sts across sleeve underarm, M1 using loose	26	27	29	30
strand between sleeve and next section;** knit across back sts; rep from * to ** at base of right sleeve; knit across	49	50	54	56
right front sts.	26	27	29	30
sts	113	116	124	128
Option 1: Stockinette Body				
Work even in St st until back measures inches from cast-on edge at center back, or ¾ inch less than desired length, ending with a WS row.	11	11	11½	11½
Dec row (RS): Knit and dec sts evenly spaced across row.	11	12	12	13
sts	102	104	112	115
Knit 6 rows.				
Bind off loosely in knit on WS.				
Option 2: Baby Bricks Body				
Work even in St st until back measures inches from cast-on edge at center back, ending with a WS row.	7	7	7½	7½
Next 4 rows: Knit, and on last row inc st(s).	0	1	1	1
sts	113	117	125	129
Change to Baby Bricks pat; work even until back measures inches from cast-on edge at center back, or ¾ inch less than desired length, ending with a WS row.	11	11	11½	11½
Dec row (RS): Knit, dec sts evenly spaced across row.	11	12	12	13
sts	102	105	113	116
Knit 6 rows.				
Bind off loosely in knit on WS.				
Neckband				
With RS facing and beg at center front, pick up and knit sts around neck edge.	65	68	70	72
Knit 2 rows.				
Bind off loosely in knit on WS.				

Tip

To aid in even distribution of sts, fold sweater in half at neck and place marker at center back. Half of neckband sts will be picked up on each side between marker and front edge.

Button Band *(left front for girls; right front for boys)*

With RS of front edge facing, pick up and knit sts evenly spaced along front edge (approx 3 sts for every 4 rows). 48 48 52 52

Knit 6 rows, ending with a RS row.

Bind off loosely in knit on WS.

> **Tip**
>
> Everyone's tension is different. The band should lie flat without ruffling or buckling the front edge of the sweater. If the band does not lie flat, rip it out and adjust the number of sts, making note of the final number.

Buttonhole Band

With RS facing, pick up and knit the same number of sts as for button band.

For Girls

Rows 1 and 2: Knit.

Row 3 (Buttonhole row, WS): K2, ssk, 2yo, k2tog, [k , ssk, 2yo, k2tog] 4 times, k2. 6 6 7 7

Row 4: Knit across, working (k1, p1) into each 2yo.

Rows 5 and 6: Knit.

Bind off loosely in knit on WS.

For Boys

Rows 1–3: Knit.

Row 4 (Buttonhole row, RS): K2, ssk, 2yo, k2tog, (k , ssk, 2yo, k2tog) 4 times, k2—5 buttonholes made. 6 6 7 7

Row 5: Knit across, working (k1, p1) into each 2yo.

Row 6: Knit.

Bind off loosely in knit on WS.

> **Tip**
>
> If you changed the number of sts in the front bands, you will need to recalculate the buttonhole placement.

Finishing

Weave in ends. Block lightly.

Using matching sewing thread, sew on buttons and backer buttons.

Congratulations! You can now tell the world, "I knit my first cardigan!" •

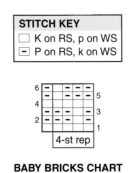

STITCH KEY
☐ K on RS, p on WS
⊟ P on RS, k on WS

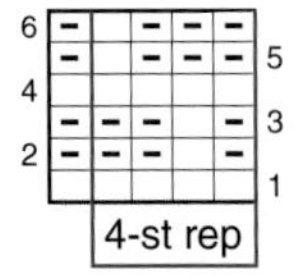

BABY BRICKS CHART

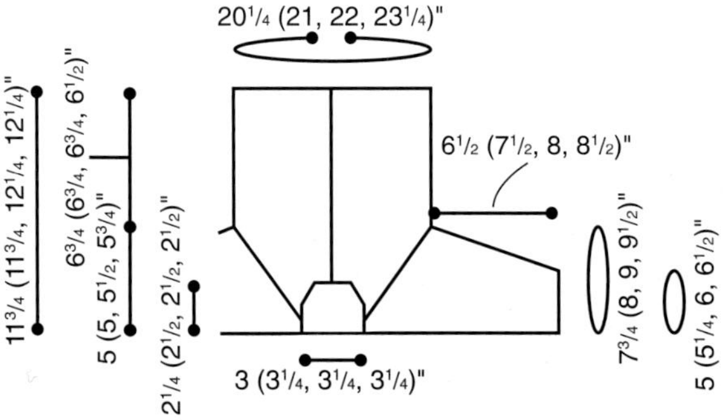

Basket Weave Basic

This adult basic top-down raglan cardigan is perfect for the beginning knitter. Choose the options that flatter your figure.

Skill Level
Easy

	Small	Medium	Large	X-Large	2X-Large	3X-Large
Sizes						
Adult with standard fit	32–34	36–38	40–42	44–46	48–50	52–54
Finished Measurements						
Chest (buttoned): inches	37	41	45	49	53	57
Length: inches	23	24	25	26	26	26
Materials						
Berroco Vintage (worsted weight; 50% acrylic/40% wool/10% nylon; 217 yds/100g per skein): skeins fennel #5175 (4 MEDIUM)	6	8	9	10	11	12

Materials
- Berroco Vintage (worsted weight; 50% acrylic/40% wool/10% nylon; 217 yds/100g per skein): skeins fennel #5175
- Size 7 (4.5mm) 40-inch circular needle or size needed to obtain gauge
- 6 (1-inch) buttons #93262 from JHB International
- 6 (⅝-inch) backer buttons #40802 from JHB International
- Stitch markers
- Piece of smooth, lightweight scrap yarn about 5 inches long in a contrasting color
- Sewing thread to match main color

Gauge
20 sts and 25 rows = 4 inches in St st.
To save time, take time to check gauge.

Special Abbreviations
Make 1 (M1): Insert LH needle from front to back under the running thread between the last st worked and next st on LH needle; knit into the back of resulting loop.
Double yarn over (2yo): Yo twice; on next row, work (k1, p1) into 2yo.

Slip marker (sm): Slip marker from LH to RH needle.

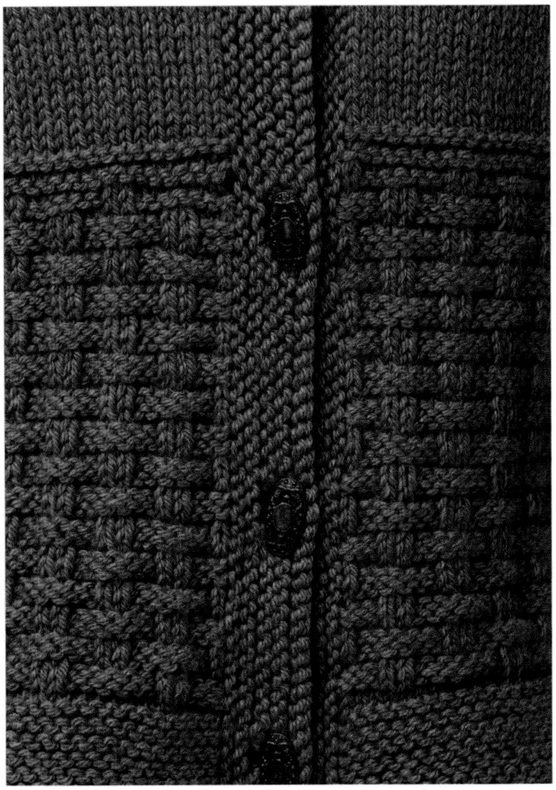

Pattern Stitch

Note: *A chart is provided for those preferring to work pat st from a chart.*

Basket Weave (multiple of 8 sts + 2)

Row 1 (RS): K2, *p6, k2; rep from * to end.

Row 2: P2, *k6, p2, rep from * to end.

Row 3: Knit.

Row 4: K2, *k2, p2, k4; rep from * to end.

Row 5: *P4, k2, p2, rep from * to last 2 sts, p2.

Row 6: Purl.

Rep Rows 1–6 for pat.

Pattern Note

Before beginning, be sure to read the Before You Get Started section for complete information on top-down architecture, seaming techniques, size selection and more.

Yoke

Cast on ___ sts.	39	43	45	49	52	59
Set-up row (WS): P ___ right front sts, pm;	2	2	2	2	2	3
p ___ right sleeve sts, pm;	5	5	5	5	5	7
p ___ back sts, pm;	25	29	31	35	38	37
p ___ left sleeve sts, pm;	5	5	5	5	5	7
p ___ left front sts.	2	2	2	2	2	3
Row 1 (RS): [Knit to 1 st before marker, kfb, sm, kfb] 4 times, knit to end. ***Note:*** *Each completed Row 1 adds 8 sts.*						
___ sts	47	51	53	57	60	67
Row 2: Purl.						
Rep Rows 1 and 2 ___ more times.	6	6	6	4	6	5
___ sts	95	99	101	89	108	107

Shape Front Neck Edge

Row 3 (RS): Kfb, [knit to 1 st before marker, kfb, sm, kfb] 4 times, knit to last 2 sts, kfb, k1. ***Note:*** *Each completed Row 3 adds 10 sts.*						
___ sts	105	109	111	99	118	117
Row 4: Purl.						
Rep Rows 3 and 4 ___ more times.	3	3	4	6	6	7
___ sts	135	139	151	159	178	187

Next row (RS): Cast on sts, [knit to 1 st before marker, kfb, sm, kfb] 4 times, knit to end.	3	5	5	5	5	5
sts	146	152	164	172	191	200
Next row (WS): Cast on sts, purl to end. The neck edge shaping is now complete.	3	5	5	5	5	5
sts	149	157	169	177	196	205

Tip: Even though you did a tension swatch, now is the time to double check your gauge. Why? When you worked your swatch, you were concentrating on tension; now that you're working on the sweater itself, your mind is on other aspects of your knitting. Gauge can reflect that difference. Measure your gauge at least ¾ inch below the needle across 4 inches on the sweater back. If gauge is different, bite the bullet and reknit after switching to the appropriate needle size.

Work Rows 1 and 2 more times.	11	14	17	18	16	22
sts	237	269	305	321	324	381
All Sizes Except 3X-Large						
Row 5: [Knit to 1 st before marker, kfb, sm, knit to next marker, sm, kfb] twice, knit to end. ***Note:*** *Each completed Row 5 inc fronts and back only, adding 4 sts.*						
sts	241	273	309	325	328	
Row 6: Purl.						
Work Rows 5 and 6 more times.	7	5	2	2	4	
sts	265	289	313	329	340	
Sizes Large (X-Large, 2X-Large, 3X-Large) Only						
Row 7: [Knit to 2 sts before marker, kfb twice, sm, knit to next marker, sm, kfb twice] twice, knit to end. ***Note:*** *Row 7 inc fronts and back only, adding 8 sts.*						
sts			321	337	348	389
Row 8: Purl.						
Work 1 row even, or until center back measures at least inches from cast-on edge, ending with a RS row.	9½	10	10½	11	11½	12
sts each front	39	42	46	49	51	55
sts each sleeve	51	57	65	67	67	81
back sts	85	91	99	105	112	117

Divide for Right Sleeve

With WS facing, purl across right front to first marker and right sleeve to 2nd marker; remove this marker and turn.

Right Sleeve

*Cast on ____ sts and knit to marker, adding a boundary line near center of sleeve; remove this marker and turn.	4	5	6	8	10	12
Cast on ____ sts and purl across sleeve.	4	5	6	8	10	12
____ sleeve sts	59	67	77	83	87	105
Option 1: Standard Sleeve Length: ____ inches to underarm	16½	17½	18	18	18½	18½
*Work back and forth in St st across sleeve sts until sleeve measures ____ inch(es) from boundary line, ending with a WS row.	1½	1	¾	1½	1½	½
Dec row (RS): K1, k2tog, knit to last 3 sts, ssk, k1. ____ sts	57	65	75	81	85	103
*Work ____ inch even, ending with a WS row; work Dec row.	¾	¾	¾	½	½	½
Rep from * ____ more times.	13	16	20	21	22	30
____ sts	31	33	35	39	41	43
Work even until sleeve measures ____ inches from boundary line or 1½ inches less than desired length, ending with a WS row.	14½	15½	16	16	16½	16½
Dec row (RS): Knit, dec ____ sts evenly spaced across row.	3	3	3	4	4	4
____ sts	28	30	32	35	37	39

Knit 8 rows, ending with a RS row.

Bind off loosely kwise on WS.

Cut yarn, leaving a long tail. Use this tail to sew sleeve seam using mattress st.

Option 2: Custom Sleeve Length

Your measurement from wrist to underarm ____ inches

Subtract 2 inches (ease + cuff) = A ____

____ number of dec = B	14	17	21	22	23	31

Divide A by (B + 1) = ____ how far between dec in inches = C

Work back and forth in St st across sleeve sts until sleeve measures ____ inches (C) from boundary line, ending with a WS row.

Dec row (RS): K1, k2tog, knit to last 3 sts, ssk, k1.						
sts	57	65	75	81	85	103
*Work inch even (C), ending with a WS row; work Dec row.						
Rep from * more times.	13	16	20	21	22	30
sts	31	33	35	39	41	43
Work even until sleeve measures inches (A) from boundary line or 1½ inches less than desired length, ending with a WS row.						
Dec row (RS): Knit, dec sts evenly spaced across row.	3	3	3	4	4	4
sts	28	30	32	35	37	39

Knit 8 rows, ending with a RS row.

Bind off loosely kwise on WS.

Cut yarn, leaving a long tail. Use this tail to sew sleeve seam using mattress st.

Divide for Left Sleeve

With WS facing, attach yarn to sweater back adjacent to base of completed right sleeve. Purl across back sts to first marker and left sleeve sts to 2nd marker; remove this marker and turn.

Left Sleeve *(both options)*

Complete left sleeve same as right sleeve.

Body

With WS facing, attach yarn to back of sweater adjacent to base of completed left sleeve. Purl across left front sts.

Unification row (RS): Knit across left front sts;	39	42	46	49	51	55
*M1 using loose strand between previous section and sleeve; pick up and knit sts across underarm of sleeve to seam,	3	5	7	8	10	12
pm, pick up and knit sts across rest of sleeve underarm; M1 using loose strand between sleeve and next section;**	3	5	7	8	10	12
knit across back sts; rep from * to ** at base of right sleeve;	85	91	99	105	112	117
knit across right front sts.	39	42	46	49	51	55
sts	179	199	219	239	258	279

Option 1: Stockinette Body Without Waist Shaping (easiest)						
Work even until back measures inches from cast-on edge at center back, or 1½ inches less than desired length, ending with a WS row.	21½	22½	23½	24½	24½	24½
Dec row (RS): Knit, dec sts evenly spaced across row.	18	20	22	24	26	29
sts	161	179	197	215	232	251
Knit 8 rows.						
Bind off loosely in knit on WS.						
Option 2: Stockinette Body With Waist Shaping (easy)						
Work even until back measures inches from cast-on edge (or 4 inches above waist), ending with a WS row.	13	13¼	13½	13¾	14	14
Dec row (RS): [Knit to 3 sts before marker, k2tog, k1, sm, k1, ssk] twice, knit to end.						
sts	175	195	215	235	254	275
Rep Dec row [every 2 inches] twice more.						
sts	167	187	207	227	146	267
Work 1 inch even, ending with a WS row.						
Inc row (RS): [Knit to 2 sts before marker, kfb, k1, sm, kfb] twice, knit to end.						
sts	171	191	211	231	250	271
Rep Inc row [every inch] twice more.						
sts	179	199	219	239	258	279
Work even until back measures inches from cast-on edge at center back, or 1½ inches less than desired length, ending with a WS row.	21½	22½	23½	24½	24½	24½
Dec row (RS): Knit, dec sts evenly spaced across row.	18	20	22	24	26	28
sts	161	179	197	215	232	251
Knit 8 rows, ending with a RS row.						
Bind off loosely in knit on WS.						
Option 3: Basket Weave Body Without Waist Shaping (easy)						
Work even in St st until back measures inches from cast-on edge at center back, ending with a WS row.	14¼	15¼	16¼	17¼	17¼	17¼
Next 4 rows: Knit, and on last row, inc or dec sts evenly spaced across.	Dec 1	Inc 3	Dec 1	Inc 3	0	Inc 3
st(s)	178	202	218	242	258	282

Change to Basket Weave pat; work even until back measures inches from cast-on edge at center back, or 1½ inches less than desired length, ending with Row 6.	21½	22½	23½	24½	24½	24½
Dec row (RS): Knit, dec sts evenly spaced across row.	18	20	22	24	26	28
sts	160	182	197	218	232	254

Knit 8 rows.

Bind off loosely in knit on WS.

Neckband

With RS facing and beg at center front, pick up and knit sts around neck edge.	77	84	86	92	96	101

Tip Everyone's tension is different. The band should lie flat without ruffling or buckling the front edge of the sweater. If the band does not lie flat, rip it out and adjust the number of sts, making note of the final number.

Work 1 inch in garter st, ending with a RS row.

Bind off loosely in knit on WS.

Button Band *(left front for women; right front for men)*

With RS of front edge facing, pick up and knit sts evenly spaced along front edge (approx 3 sts for every 4 rows).	100	106	111	116	118	118

Knit 8 rows.

Bind off loosely in knit on WS.

Buttonhole Band

With RS facing, pick up and knit the same number of sts as for button band.

For Women

Rows 1–4: Knit.

Row 5 (Buttonhole row, WS): K3, ssk, 2yo, k2tog, [k , ssk, 2yo, k2tog] 5 times, knit to end.	14	15	16	17	17	17

Row 6: [Knit to 2yo, (k1, p1) into 2yo] 6 times, knit to end.

Rows 7 and 8: Knit.

Bind off loosely in knit on WS.

For Men

Rows 1–3: Knit.

Row 4 (Buttonhole row, RS): K3, ssk, 2yo, k2tog, (k , ssk, 2yo, k2tog) 5 times, knit to end.

14 15 16 17 17 17

Row 5: [Knit to 2yo, (k1, p1) into 2yo] 6 times, knit to end.

Rows 6–8: Knit.

Bind off loosely in knit on WS.

Finishing

Weave in ends. Block lightly.

Using matching sewing thread, sew on buttons and backer buttons.

You did it! Your new cardigan is ready to wear with pride. •

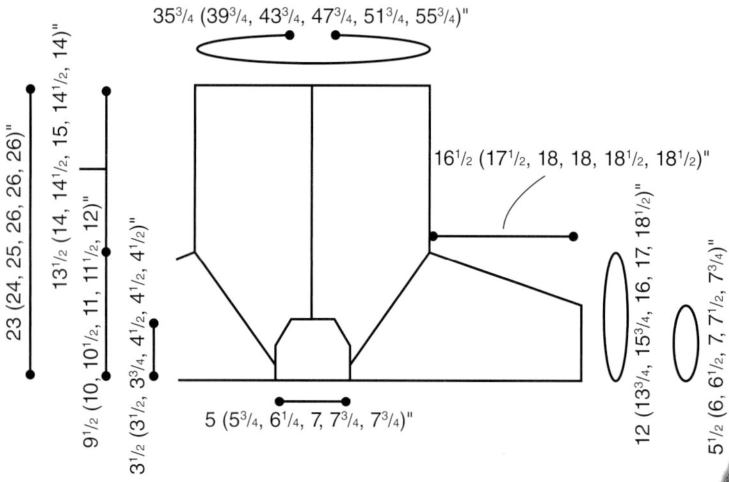

STITCH KEY

☐ K on RS, p on WS

⊟ P on RS, k on WS

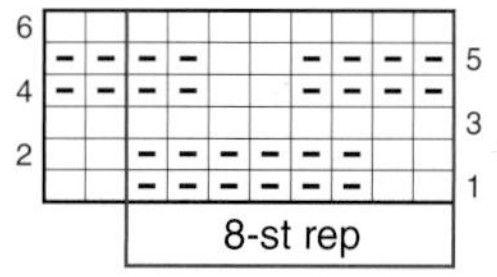

BASKET WEAVE CHART

Kisses & Hugs

The XOX form of this cable gives it the name Kisses & Hugs. What a wonderful way to show your affection and warmth for a little one!

Skill Level

Intermediate

Sizes

Baby with standard fit

Finished Measurements

Chest (buttoned): inches

Length: inches

Materials

- SMC Baby Wool (fingering weight; 100% superwash merino wool; 93 yds/25g per ball): balls white #00001 (1 SUPER FINE)

	6 mo	12 mo	18 mo	24 mo
Chest (buttoned), inches	21	21¾	22¾	24
Length, inches	11¾	11¾	12¼	12¼
SMC Baby Wool, balls	6	6	7	7

- Size 4 (3.5mm) 32-inch circular needle or 2 sizes smaller than needle used for body
- Size 5 (3.75mm) 32-inch circular needle or size needed to obtain gauge
- Cable needle
- Stitch markers
- 5 (½-inch) buttons #90548 from JHB International
- 5 (½-inch) backer buttons #40800 from JHB International
- Piece of smooth, lightweight scrap yarn about 5 inches long in a contrasting color
- Sewing thread to match sweater

Gauge

25 sts and 34 rows = 4 inches/10cm in St st on larger needles (before blocking).

24 sts and 32 rows = 4 inches/10cm (blocked).

To save time, take time to check gauge.

Tip

It is always safest to measure a swatch both before and after blocking in order to avoid nasty surprises. In this case there is a warning that the gauge will change slightly with blocking. The most critical measurement is the one taken after blocking because that is the gauge of the final result.

Special Abbreviations

2 over 2 Right Cross (2/2 RC): Sl 2 to cn and hold in back; k2, k2 from cn.

2 over 2 Left Cross (2/2 LC): Sl 2 to cn and hold in front; k2, k2 from cn.

Right Twist (RT): K2tog, but do not remove from needle; knit first st again; remove both sts from needle.

Make 1 (M1): Insert LH needle from front to back under the designated running thread between sts; knit into the back of resulting loop.

Decrease in Rib (rib2tog): K2tog or p2tog as needed to maintain the established rib pat.

Slip marker (sm): Slip marker from LH to RH needle.

Pattern Stitches

Cable (10-st panel)

Note: A chart is provided for those preferring to work pat st from a chart.

Rows 1, 5, 9 and 13 (RS): P1, k8, p1.
Row 2 and all WS rows: K1, p8, k1.
Row 3: P1, 2/2 RC, 2/2 LC, p1.
Rows 7 and 11: P1, 2/2 LC, 2/2 RC, p1.
Row 15: Rep Row 3.
Row 16: K1, p8, K1.
Rep Rows 1–16 for pat.

Twist (4-st panel)
Row 1 (WS): K1, p2, k1.
Row 2 (RS): P1, RT, p1.
Rep Rows 1 and 2 for pat.

2x2 Rib (multiple of 4 sts + 2)
Row 1 (WS): *P2, k2; rep from * to last 2 sts, p2.
Row 2 (RS): *K2, p2; rep from * to last 2 sts, k2.
Rep Rows 1 and 2 for pat.

Pattern Note

Before beginning, be sure to read the Before You Get Started section for complete information on top-down architecture, seaming techniques, size selection and more.

Yoke

Cast on sts.	41	44	46	48
Set-up row (WS): P right front sts, pm; work Twist pat	2	2	2	2
over next 4 sts, pm; p right sleeve sts, pm; work Twist	3	4	4	5
pat over next 4 sts, pm; p back sts, pm; work Twist pat	15	16	18	18
over next 4 sts, pm; p left sleeve sts, pm; work Twist pat	3	4	4	5
over next 4 sts, pm; p left front sts.	2	2	2	2
Row 1 (RS): [Knit to 2 sts before marker, kfb, k1, sm, work Twist pat Row 2, sm, kfb] 4 times, knit to end. ***Note:*** *Each completed Row 1 adds 8 sts.*				
sts	49	52	54	56
Row 2: Purl, working Twist pat between markers as established.				
Rep [Rows 1 and 2] 4 more times.				
sts	81	84	86	88

Shape Front Neck Edge

Row 3 (RS): Kfb, [knit to 2 sts before marker, kfb, k1, sm, work Twist pat, sm, kfb] 4 times, knit to last 2 sts, kfb, k1. ***Note:*** *Each completed Row 3 adds 10 sts.*				
sts	91	94	96	98
Row 4: Purl, working Twist pat between markers as established.				
Rep [Rows 3 and 4] twice more.				
sts	111	114	116	118
Next row (RS): Cast on 12 sts; working across these new sts and remainder of row, k2, work Row 1 of Cable panel, pm, [knit to 2 sts before marker, kfb, k1, sm, work Twist pat, sm, kfb] 4 times, knit to end.				
sts	131	134	136	138
Next row (WS): Cast on 12 sts; working across these new sts and remainder of row, p2, work Row 2 of Cable panel over 10 sts, pm, work in established pats to last 2 sts, p2. The neck edge shaping is now complete.				
sts	143	146	148	150
Work Rows 1 and 2 more times.	7	8	9	10
total sts	199	210	220	230
Work 1 row even or until center back measures at least	4½	4¾	5	5¼
inches from cast-on edge, ending with a RS row.				
sts each front	33	34	35	36
sts each sleeve	35	38	40	43
back sts	47	50	54	56

Divide for Right Sleeve

With WS facing and removing raglan markers when you come to them, work across right front to marker, p2, pm, purl across right sleeve sts to next marker, p2, turn. ***Note:*** *Twist pats end here and those sts are now divided among the various sweater parts.*

Right Sleeve

Cast on 3 sts; knit to marker, adding a boundary line near center of sleeve; remove this marker and turn.

sleeve sts — 40 | 43 | 45 | 48

Cast on 3 sts and purl across sleeve.

sleeve sts — 45 | 48 | 50 | 53

Work even until sleeve measures ¾ | 1 | 1½ | 1¾ inch(es) from boundary line, ending with a WS row.

Dec row (RS): K1, k2tog, knit to last 3 sts, ssk, k1.

sts — 43 | 46 | 48 | 51

[Work ¾ inch even, ending with a WS row; work Dec row] 5 times.

sts — 33 | 36 | 38 | 41

Work even until sleeve measures 5¾ | 6¾ | 7¼ | 7¾ inches from boundary line or ¾ inch less than desired length, ending with a WS row.

Dec row (RS): Knit and dec 3 | 2 | 4 | 3 sts evenly spaced across row.

sts — 30 | 34 | 34 | 38

Change to smaller needle and work 6 rows in 2x2 Rib.

Bind off loosely in rib.

Cut yarn, leaving a long tail. Use this tail to sew sleeve seam using mattress st.

Divide for Left Sleeve

With WS facing, attach yarn to back adjacent to base of completed right sleeve. Removing markers when you come to them, p2, purl across back to marker, p2, pm, p2, purl across left sleeve to marker, p2; turn.

Left Sleeve

Work as for right sleeve.

Body

With WS facing, attach yarn adjacent to base of completed left sleeve. P2, remove marker, purl across left front.

Unification row (RS): Work in established pat across 35 | 36 | 37 | 38 left front sts; *M1 using loose strand between previous section and sleeve, pick up and knit 4 sts across sleeve underarm, M1

Tip

To ensure a loose bind-off, hold the larger needle in your right hand while binding off.

using loose strand between sleeve and next section;** knit across back sts; rep from * to ** at base of right sleeve; work in established pat across right front sts.	51 35	54 36	58 37	60 38
sts	133	138	144	148
Work even until back measures inches from cast-on edge at center back, ending with a RS row.	11	11	11½	11½
Change to smaller needle; work in established Cable pat to first marker; work 2x2 Rib to next marker and dec sts evenly spaced across; work Cable to end.	7	4	6	6
sts	126	134	138	142
Work 5 rows even.				
Bind off loosely in pat.				

Neckband

With RS facing, beg at center front and using smaller needle, pick up and knit sts around neck edge.	82	82	82	82
Work 4 rows in 2x2 Rib.				
Bind off loosely in rib.				

Button Band *(left front for girls; right front for boys)*

With RS facing and using smaller needle, pick up and knit sts evenly spaced along front edge (approx 3 sts for every 4 rows).	50	50	54	54
Work 6 rows in 2x2 Rib.				
Bind off loosely in rib.				

Buttonhole Band

With RS facing and using smaller needle, pick up and knit the same number of sts as for button band.

For Girls

Rows 1 and 2: Work 2x2 Rib.				
Row 3 (Buttonhole row, WS): Work 5 sts, k2tog, yo, [work sts, rib2tog, yo] 4 times, work 3 sts—5 buttonholes made.	8	8	9	9
Rows 4–6: Work in established rib.				
Bind off loosely in knit on WS.				

For Boys

Rows 1–3: Work 2x2 Rib.				
Row 4 (Buttonhole row, RS): Work 5 sts, k2tog, yo, [work sts, rib2tog, yo] 4 times, work 3 sts—5 buttonholes made.	8	8	9	9
Rows 5 and 6: Work in established rib.				
Bind off loosely in knit on WS.				

Finishing

Weave in ends.

Block lightly.

Using matching sewing thread, sew on buttons and backer buttons.

Now it's ready—kisses and hugs for that special baby. ●

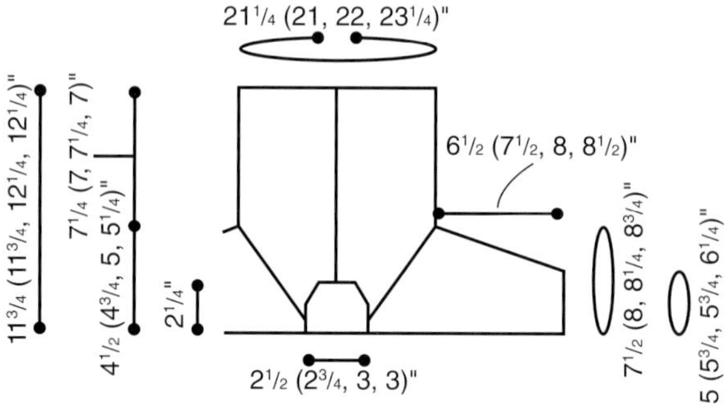

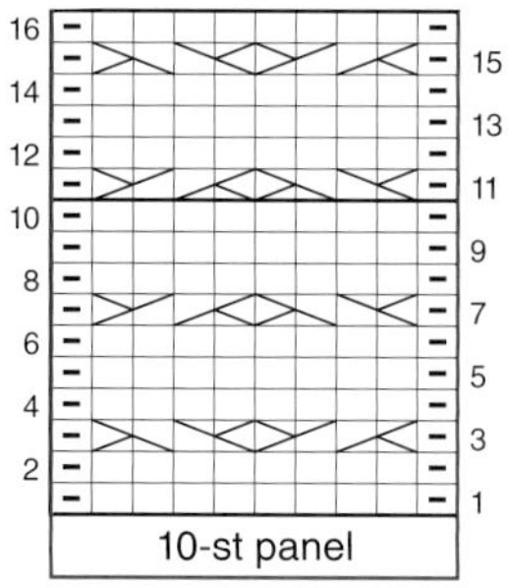

CABLE CHART

STITCH KEY
☐ K on RS, p on WS
▭ P on RS, k on WS
2/2 LC
2/2 RC

Classic Cables

Twists, cables and snuggly yarn give this sweater the look and feel everyone will want for a crisp day on the go.

Skill level
Intermediate

	Small	Medium	Large	X-Large	2X-Large	3X-Large
Sizes Adult with standard fit	32–34	36–38	40–42	44–46	48–50	52–54
Finished Measurements						
Chest (buttoned): inches	37	41	45	49	53	57
Length: inches	23	24	25	26	26	26
Materials Plymouth Encore Worsted Tweed: balls granola #1237	6	6	7	8	9	10

Materials
- Plymouth Encore Worsted Tweed (worsted weight; 75% acrylic/22% wool/3% rayon; 200 yds/100g per ball): balls granola #1237 (4 MEDIUM)
- Size 6 (4mm) 32-inch circular needle or 2 sizes smaller than needle used to obtain gauge
- Size 8 (5mm) 40-inch circular needle or size needed to obtain gauge
- Cable needle
- Stitch markers
- 6 (1-inch) buttons #64456 from JHB International
- 6 (5/8-inch) backer buttons #40802 from JHB International
- Piece of smooth, lightweight scrap yarn about 5 inches long in a contrasting color
- Sewing thread to match sweater

Gauge
20 sts and 25 rows = 4 inches/10cm in St st with larger needle.
To save time, take time to check gauge.

Special Abbreviations
2 over 2 Left Purl Cross (2/2 LPC): Sl 2 to cn and hold in front, p2, k2 from cn.

2 over 2 Right Purl Cross (2/2 RPC): Sl 2 to cn and hold in back, k2, p2 from cn.

2 over 2 Left Cross (2/2 LC): Sl 2 to cn and hold in front, k2, k2 from cn.

2 over 2 Right Cross (2/2 RC): Sl 2 to cn and hold in back, k2, k2 from cn.

Right Twist (RT): K2tog, but do not remove from needle; knit first st again; remove both sts from needle.

Left Twist (LT): Knit 2nd st through back loop but do not remove from needle; knit first st; remove both sts from needle.

Make 1 (M1): Insert LH needle from front to back under the designated running thread between sts; knit into the back of resulting loop.

Slip marker (sm): Slip marker from LH needle to RH needle.

Pattern Stitches

Note: Charts are provided for those preferring to work pat st from a chart.

Twist Pat (6-st panel)
Row 1 (WS): K1, p4, k1.
Row 2: P1, RT, LT, p1.
Rep Rows 1 and 2 for pat.

Left Cable (12-st panel)
Set-up row (RS): P1, k4, p4, k2, p1.
Row 1 (WS): K1, p2, k4, p4, k1.
Row 2: P1, k4, p2, 2/2 RPC, p1.
Row 3: K3, p2, k2, p4, k1.
Row 4: P1, 2/2 RPC, 2/2 RC, p3.
Row 5: K3, p4, k2, p2, k1.
Row 6: P1, k2, 2/2 RPC, 2/2 LPC, p1.
Row 7: K1, p2, k4, p4, k1.
Row 8: P1, 2/2 RC, p4, k2, p1.
Rep Rows 1–8 for pat.

Right Cable (12-st panel)
Row 1 (WS): K1, p4, k4, p2, k1.
Row 2 (RS): P1, 2/2 LPC, p2, k4, p1.
Row 3: K1, p4, k2, p2, k3.
Row 4: P3, 2/2 LC, 2/2 LPC, p1.
Row 5: K1, p2, k2, p4, k3.
Row 6: P1, 2/2 RPC, 2/2 LPC, k2, p1.
Row 7: K1, p4, k4, p2, k1.
Row 8: P1, k2, p4, 2/2 LC, p1.
Rep Rows 1–8 for pat.

2x2 Rib (multiple of 4 sts + 2)
Row 1 (WS): P2 *k2, p2; rep from * to end.
Row 2 (RS): K2, *p2, k2; rep from * to end.
Rep Rows 1 and 2 for pat.

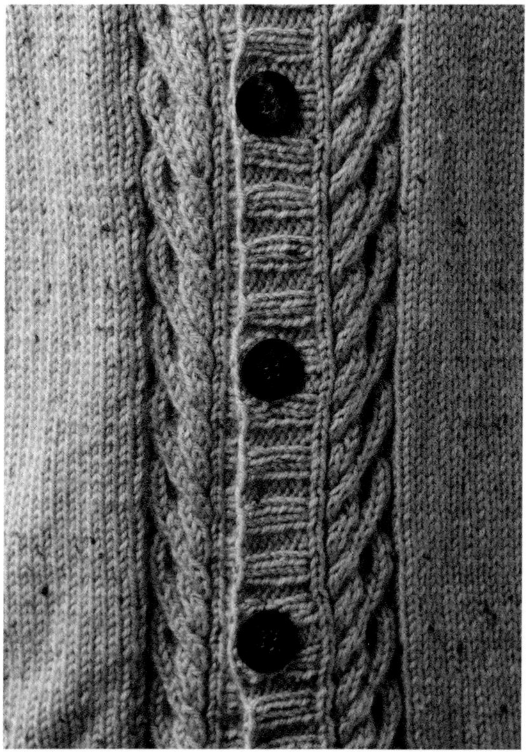

Pattern Note

Before beginning, be sure to read the Before You Get Started section for complete information on top-down architecture, seaming techniques, size selection and more.

Yoke

Cast on sts.	**51**	**51**	**57**	**57**	**64**	**65**
Set-up row (WS): P right front sts, pm; work Twist pat across next 6 sts, pm;	**2**	**2**	**2**	**2**	**2**	**2**
p right sleeve sts, pm; work Twist pat across next 6 sts, pm;	**3**	**3**	**4**	**2**	**4**	**4**
p back sts, pm; work Twist pat across next 6 sts, pm;	**17**	**17**	**21**	**25**	**28**	**29**
p left sleeve sts, pm; work Twist pat across next 6 sts, pm;	**3**	**3**	**4**	**2**	**4**	**4**
p left front sts.	**2**	**2**	**2**	**2**	**2**	**2**
Row 1 (RS): [Knit to 2 sts before marker, kfb, k1, sm, work Twist pat, sm, kfb] 4 times, knit to end. *Note: Each completed Row 1 adds 8 sts.*						
sts	**59**	**59**	**65**	**65**	**72**	**73**
Row 2: Purl, working Twist pat between markers as established.						
Rep Rows 1 and 2 more times.	**9**	**7**	**7**	**7**	**7**	**5**
sts	**131**	**115**	**121**	**121**	**128**	**113**

Shape Front Neck Edge

Row 3 (RS): Kfb, [knit to 2 sts before marker, kfb, k1, sm, work Twist pat, sm, kfb] 4 times, knit to last 2 sts, kfb, k1. ***Note:** Each completed Row 3 adds 10 sts.*						
sts	**141**	**125**	**131**	**131**	**138**	**123**
Row 4: Purl, working Twist pat between markers as established.						
Rep Rows 3 and 4 more times.	**0**	**2**	**3**	**5**	**5**	**7**
sts	**141**	**145**	**161**	**181**	**188**	**193**
Next row (RS): Cast on 14 sts; working across these new sts and remainder of row, k2, work Set-up row of Left Cable across 12 sts, pm, [knit to 2 sts before marker, kfb, k1, sm, work Twist pat, sm, kfb] 4 times, knit to end.						
sts	**163**	**167**	**183**	**203**	**210**	**215**
Next row (WS): Cast on 14 sts; working across these new sts and remainder of row, p2, work Row 1 of Right Cable across 12 sts, pm, work in established pats to last 2 sts, p2. ***Note:** The neck edge shaping is now complete.*						
sts	**177**	**181**	**197**	**217**	**224**	**229**
Maintaining established pats, inc on RS rows as for Row 1 more times, ending with a WS row.	**10**	**12**	**15**	**17**	**14**	**21**
sts	**257**	**277**	**317**	**353**	**336**	**397**
Row 5: [Work to 2 sts before marker, kfb, k1, sm, work Twist pat, sm, knit to next marker, sm, work Twist pat, sm, kfb] twice, knit to end. ***Note:** Each completed Row 5 inc fronts and back only, adding 4 sts.*						
sts	**261**	**281**	**321**	**357**	**340**	**401**
Row 6: Work even.						
Work Rows 5 and 6 more time(s).	**5**	**6**	**4**	**3**	**6**	**1**
sts	**281**	**305**	**337**	**353**	**364**	**405**
Work 1 row even, or until center back measures at least inches from cast-on edge, ending with a RS row.	**9½**	**10**	**10½**	**11**	**11½**	**12**
sts each front	**45**	**50**	**53**	**58**	**58**	**62**
sts each sleeve	**47**	**51**	**60**	**66**	**62**	**76**
back sts	**73**	**79**	**87**	**97**	**100**	**105**
sts in Twist pat (6 sts each)	**24**	**24**	**24**	**24**	**24**	**24**

***Note:** Twist pats end here and those sts will now be added to the adjacent sweater parts.*

Divide for Right Sleeve

With WS facing, work across right front to marker, remove marker, p3, pm, p3, purl across right sleeve to marker, remove marker, p3; turn.

Right Sleeve

Row 1 (RS): Cast on sts; knit to marker, adding a boundary line near center of sleeve; remove this marker and turn.	4	5	6	8	10	12
Row 2: Cast on sts and purl across sleeve.	4	5	6	8	10	12
sleeve sts	61	67	78	88	88	106
Option 1: Standard Sleeve Length: inches to underarm	16½	17½	18	18	18½	18½
Work sleeve even until sleeve measures inch(es) from boundary line, ending with a WS row.	1½	1	¾	1½	1½	1½
Dec row (RS): K1, k2tog, knit to last 3 sts, ssk, k1.						
sts	59	65	76	86	86	104
*Work inch even, ending with a WS row; work Dec row.	¾	¾	¾	½	½	½
Rep from * more times.	13	16	20	21	22	30
sts	33	33	36	44	42	44
Work even until sleeve measures inches from boundary line or 2 inches less than desired length, ending with a WS row.	14½	15½	16	16	16½	16½
Dec row (RS): Knit and dec sts evenly spaced across row.	3	3	2	6	4	2
sts	30	30	34	38	38	42

Change to smaller needle; work in 2x2 Rib for 2 inches.

Bind off loosely in rib.

Cut yarn, leaving a long tail.

Use this tail to sew sleeve seam using mattress st.

> **Tip**
>
> To ensure a loose bind-off, hold the larger needle in your right hand while binding off.

Option 2: Custom Sleeve Length

Your measurement from wrist to underarm inches

Subtract 2 inches = A

number of dec = B	14	17	21	22	23	31

Divide A by (B + 1) = how far between dec in inches = C

Work sleeve even until sleeve measures inch (C) from boundary line, ending with a WS row.

Dec row (RS): K1, k2tog, knit to last 3 sts, ssk, k1.						
sts	59	65	76	86	86	104
*Work inch (C) even, ending with a WS row; work Dec row.						
Rep from * more times.	13	16	20	21	22	30
sts	33	33	36	44	42	44
Work even until sleeve measures inches (A) from boundary line or 2 inches less than desired length, ending with a WS row.						
Dec row (RS): Knit and dec sts evenly spaced across row.	3	3	2	6	4	2
sts	30	30	34	38	38	42

Change to smaller needle; work in 2x2 Rib for 2 inches.

Bind off loosely in rib.

Cut yarn, leaving a long tail.

Use this tail to sew sleeve seam using mattress st.

Divide for Left Sleeve

With WS facing, attach yarn adjacent to base of completed right sleeve, p3, remove marker, purl across back to marker, remove marker, p3, pm, p3, purl across left sleeve sts to marker, remove marker, p3; turn.

Left Sleeve *(both options)*

Work same as for right sleeve.

Body

With WS facing, attach yarn adjacent to base of completed left sleeve; p3, remove marker, work across left front.

Unification row (RS): Work in established pats across left front sts;	48	53	56	61	61	65
*M1 using loose strand between previous section and sleeve, pick up and knit sts across underarm of sleeve to seam,	3	5	6	7	10	12
pm for side, pick up and knit sts across rest of sleeve underarm, M1 using loose strand between sleeve and next section;**	3	5	6	7	10	12
knit across back sts; rep from * to ** at base of right sleeve;	79	85	93	103	106	111
work in established pats across right front sts.	48	53	56	61	61	65
sts	191	215	233	257	272	293

Option 1: Stockinette Body Without Waist Shaping						
Work even until back measures inches from cast-on edge at center back, or 2 inches less than desired length, ending with a WS row.	**21**	**22**	**23**	**24**	**24**	**24**
Ribbing						
Row 1 (RS): Knit and dec st(s) evenly across row.	**1**	**1**	**1**	**1**	**0**	**1**
sts	**194**	**214**	**234**	**254**	**274**	**294**
Row 2 (WS): Change to smaller needle; work in established pat to first cable marker; work 2x2 Rib to next cable marker, work established pat to end.						
Work even for 2 inches.						
Bind off loosely in pat.						
Option 2: Body With Waist Shaping						
Work even until back measures inches from cast-on edge, or 4 inches above waist, ending with a WS row.	**13**	**13¼**	**13½**	**13¾**	**14**	**14**
Dec row (RS): [Work to 3 sts before side marker, k2tog, k1, sm, k1, ssk] twice, work to end.						
sts	**177**	**194**	**217**	**234**	**253**	**270**
Rep Dec row every 2 inches twice more.						
sts	**169**	**186**	**209**	**226**	**245**	**262**
Work 1 inch even, ending with a WS row.						
Inc row (RS): [Work to 2 sts before side marker, kfb, k1, sm, kfb] twice, work to end.						
sts	**173**	**190**	**213**	**230**	**249**	**266**
Rep Inc row every inch twice more.						
sts	**191**	**198**	**221**	**238**	**257**	**274**
Work even until back measures inches from cast-on edge at center back, or 2 inches less than desired length, ending with a WS row.	**21**	**22**	**23**	**24**	**24**	**24**
Complete ribbing as for Option 1.						
Neckband						
With RS facing, beg at center front and using smaller needle, pick up and knit sts around neck edge.	**94**	**94**	**98**	**98**	**102**	**102**
Work 1 inch in 2x2 Rib.						
Bind off loosely in rib.						

Button Band *(left front for women; right front for men)*

With RS facing and using smaller needle, pick up and knit sts evenly spaced along front edge (approx 3 sts for every 4 rows).

102   106   110   114   114   114

Work 2x2 Rib for 8 rows (should measure approx 1¼–1½ inches), ending with a RS row.

Bind off loosely in rib.

Buttonhole Band

With RS facing and using smaller needle, pick up and knit the same number of sts as for button band.

For Women

Rows 1–4: Work in 2x2 Rib.

Row 5 (Buttonhole row, WS): Work 5 sts, bind off 3, [work sts (includes st rem on RH needle after bind-off), bind off 3] 5 times, work to end—6 buttonholes made.

14   15   16   17   17   17

Row 6: [Work to bound-off sts, cast on 3 sts] 6 times, work to end.

Rows 7–9: Work in established rib.

Bind off loosely in rib.

For Men

Rows 1–5: Work in 2x2 Rib.

Row 6 (Buttonhole row, RS): Work 5 sts, bind off 3, [work sts (includes st rem on RH needle after bind-off), bind off 3] 5 times, work to end—6 buttonholes made.

14   15   16   17   17   17

Row 7: [Work to bound-off sts, cast on 3 sts] 6 times, work to end.

Rows 8 and 9: Work in established rib.

Bind off loosely in rib.

Finishing

Weave in ends.

Block lightly.

Using matching sewing thread, sew on buttons and backer buttons.

Congratulations! Isn't it beautiful? Now you're ready for a chilly day. •

Tip

If you changed the number of sts in the front bands, you will need to recalculate the buttonhole placement.

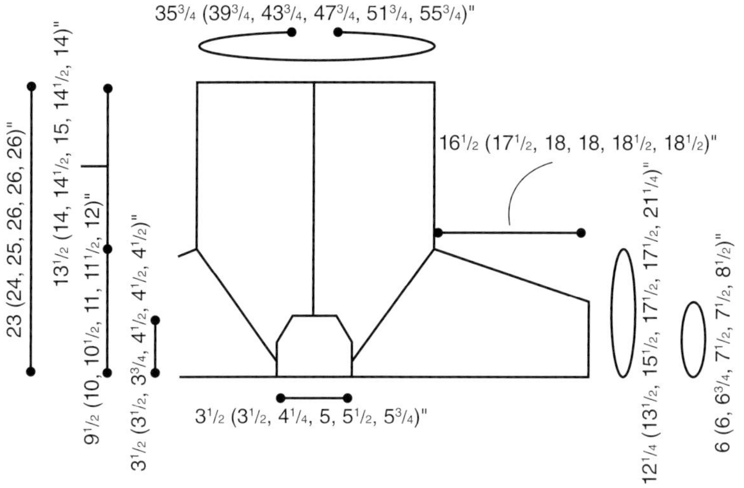

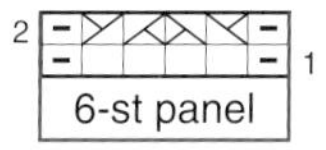

TWIST PAT CHART

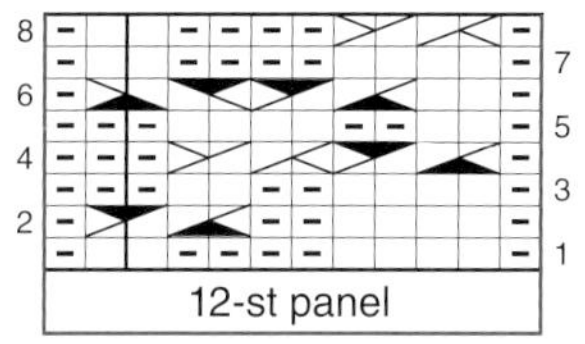

LEFT CABLE CHART

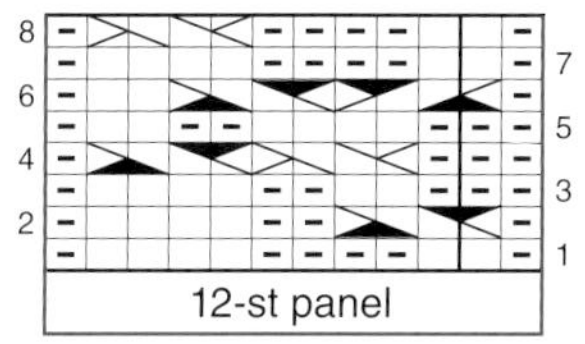

RIGHT CABLE CHART

STITCH KEY

- K on RS, p on WS
- P on RS, k on WS
- RT
- LT
- 2/2 RC
- 2/2 LC
- 2/2 RPC
- 2/2 LPC

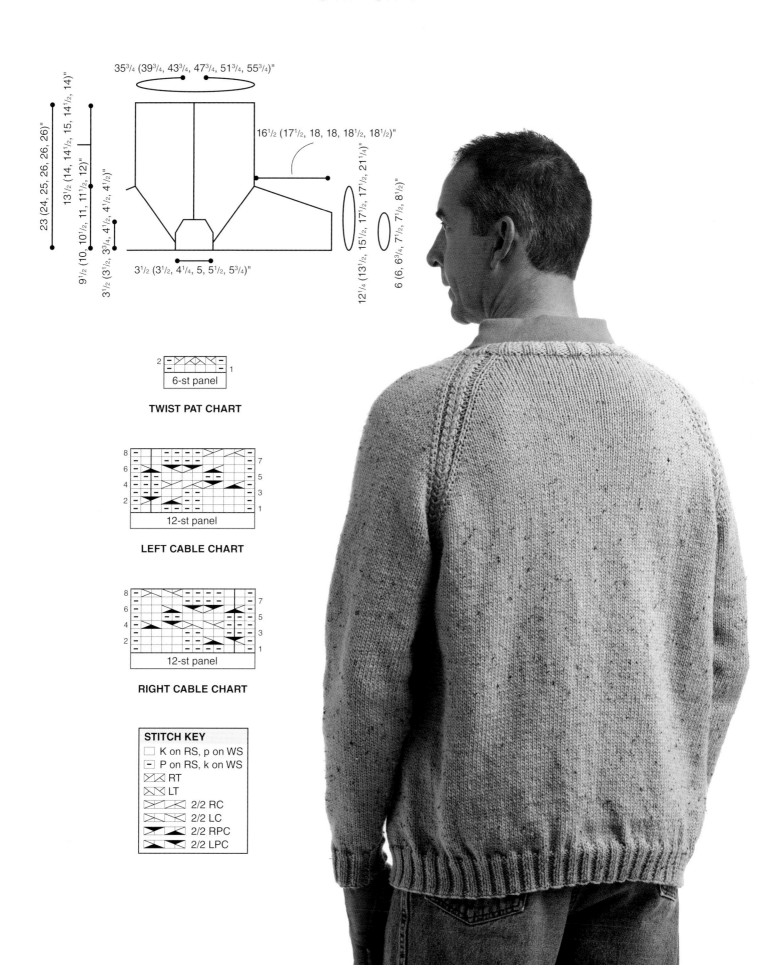

Sweet & Simple Lace

Boy or girl, every baby needs a cardigan with a hint of lace for a warm touch on cool evenings.

Skill level

Intermediate

Sizes

Baby with standard fit	6 mo	12 mo	18 mo	24 mo

Finished Measurements

	6 mo	12 mo	18 mo	24 mo
Chest (buttoned): inches	21	21¾	22¾	24
Length: inches	11¾	11¾	12¼	12¼

Materials

	6 mo	12 mo	18 mo	24 mo
Plymouth Dreambaby DK (DK weight; 50% acrylic/50% nylon; 183 yds/50g per ball): balls lime/blue/purple #209 or blue spots #301 (3 LIGHT)	2	2	3	3

- Size 6 (4mm) 32-inch circular needle or size needed to obtain gauge
- Stitch markers
- 5 (½-inch] buttons #11146 from JHB International
- 5 (½-inch) backer buttons #40800 from JHB International
- Piece of smooth, lightweight scrap yarn about 5 inches long in a contrasting color
- Sewing thread to match main color

Gauge

22 sts and 28 rows = 4 inches/10cm in St st.
To save time, take time to check gauge.

Special Abbreviations

Make 1 (M1): Insert LH needle from front to back under the designated running thread between sts; knit into the back of resulting loop.

Slip marker (sm): Slip marker from LH needle to RH needle.

Pattern Stitches

Note: A chart is provided for those preferring to work pat st from a chart.

Crest of the Wave (multiple of 11 sts + 2) *Shown on model*

Rows 1, 3, 5 and 7 (RS): K1, *[k2tog] twice, [yo, k1] 3 times, yo, [ssk] twice, rep from * to last st, k1.

Rows 2, 4, 6 and 8: Purl.

Rows 9–12: Knit.

Rep Rows 1–12 for pat.

Eyelets (multiple of 6 sts + 2) *Shown on swatch*

Row 1 (RS): K1, *k4, k2tog, yo; rep from * to last st, k1.

Row 2 and all WS rows: Purl.

Row 3: K1, *k2, k2tog, yo, k2; rep from * to last st, k1.

Row 5: K1, *k2tog, yo, k4; rep from * to last st, k1.

Row 6: Purl.

Rep Rows 1–6 for pat.

Pattern Note

Before beginning, be sure to read the Before You Get Started section for complete information on top-down architecture, seaming techniques, size selection and more.

Yoke

Cast on sts.	31	34	36	38
Set-up row (WS): P right front sts, pm,	2	2	2	2
p right sleeve sts, pm,	5	6	7	8
p back sts, pm,	17	18	18	18
p left sleeve sts, pm,	5	6	7	8
p left front sts.	2	2	2	2

Row 1 (RS): [Knit to 1 st before marker, yo, k1, sm, k1, yo] 4 times, knit to end. ***Note:** Each completed Row 1 adds 8 sts.*

sts	39	42	44	46

Row 2: Purl.

Rep [Rows 1 and 2] twice more.

sts	55	58	60	62

Shape Front Neck Edge

Row 3 (RS): Kfb, [knit to 1 st before marker, yo, k1, sm, k1, yo] 4 times, knit to last 2 sts, kfb, k1. ***Note:*** *Each completed Row 3 adds 10 sts.*				
sts	**65**	**68**	**70**	**72**
Row 4: Purl.				
Rep Rows 3 and 4 times more—	**3**	**4**	**4**	**4**
sts	**95**	**108**	**110**	**112**
Next row (RS): Cast on 4 sts, [knit to 1 st before marker, yo, k1, sm, k1, yo] 4 times, knit to end.				
sts	**107**	**120**	**122**	**124**
Next row (WS): Cast on 4 sts, purl to end.				
sts	**111**	**124**	**126**	**128**
Note: *The neck edge shaping is now complete.*				
Work Rows 1 and 2 more times.	**8**	**7**	**9**	**10**
total sts	**175**	**180**	**198**	**208**
Work 1 row even or until center back measures at least inches from cast-on edge, ending with a RS row.	**5**	**5**	**5½**	**5¾**
sts each front	**26**	**27**	**29**	**30**
sts each sleeve	**37**	**38**	**43**	**46**
back sts	**49**	**50**	**54**	**56**

Divide for Right Sleeve

With WS facing, purl across right front to first marker and right sleeve to 2nd marker; remove this marker and turn.

Right Sleeve

Row 1 (RS): Cast on 3 sts and knit to marker, adding a boundary line near center of sleeve; remove this marker and turn.				
sleeve sts	**40**	**41**	**46**	**49**
Row 2: Cast on 3 sts and purl across sleeve.				
sleeve sts	**43**	**44**	**49**	**52**
Work even until sleeve measures inch(es) from boundary line, ending with a WS row.	**¾**	**1**	**1½**	**1¾**
Dec row (RS): K1, k2tog, knit to last 3 sts, ssk, k1.				
sts	**41**	**42**	**47**	**50**
[Work ¾ inch even, ending with a WS row; work Dec row] 5 times.				
sts	**31**	**32**	**37**	**40**
Work even until sleeve measures inches from boundary line or ¾ inch less than desired length, ending with a WS row.	**5¾**	**6¾**	**7¼**	**7¾**
Dec row (RS): Knit and dec sts evenly spaced across row.	**3**	**3**	**4**	**4**
sts	**28**	**29**	**33**	**36**

Knit 6 rows.

Bind off loosely in knit on WS.

Cut yarn, leaving a long tail. Use this tail to sew sleeve seam using mattress st.

Divide for Left Sleeve

With WS facing, attach yarn to sweater back adjacent to base of completed right sleeve. Purl across back sts to first marker and left sleeve sts to 2nd marker; remove this marker and turn.

Left Sleeve

Complete as for right sleeve.

Body

With WS facing, attach yarn to back of sweater adjacent to base of completed left sleeve. Purl across left front.

Unification row (RS): Knit across [ ] left front sts; *M1 using loose strand between previous section and sleeve, pick up and knit 4 sts across sleeve underarm, M1 using loose strand between sleeve and next section,** knit across	**26**	**27**	**29**	**30**
[ ] back sts, rep from * to ** at base of right sleeve, knit	**49**	**50**	**54**	**56**
across [ ] right front sts.	**26**	**27**	**29**	**30**
[ ] sts	**113**	**116**	**124**	**128**

Option 1: Body for Crest of the Wave Lace

Work even until back measures [ ] inches from cast-on edge at center back, ending with a WS row.	7¼	7¼	7¾	7¾
Knit 4 rows and on last row, inc or dec [ ] st(s) evenly spaced across.	**Dec 1**	**Dec 4**	**Dec 1**	**Inc 6**
[ ] sts	**112**	**112**	**123**	**134**
Change to Crest of the Wave pat; work even until back measures approx [ ] inches from cast-on edge at center back, or ¾ inch less than desired length, ending with Row 8.	**11½**	**11½**	**12**	**12**

Knit 7 rows.

Bind off loosely in knit on WS.

Option 2: Body for Eyelets Lace

Work even until back measures [ ] inches from cast-on edge at center back, ending with a WS row.	7¼	7¼	7½	7½
Knit 4 rows and on last row, inc or dec [ ] sts evenly spaced across.	**Dec 3**	**0**	**Dec 2**	**0**
[ ] sts	**110**	**116**	**122**	**128**

Change to Eyelets pat; work even until back measures approx inches from cast-on edge at center back, or ¾ inch less than desired length, ending with a WS row.	**11½**	**11½**	**12**	**12**
Dec row (RS): Knit and dec sts evenly spaced across row.	**11**	**12**	**12**	**13**
sts	**99**	**104**	**110**	**115**

Knit 6 rows, ending with a RS row.

Bind off loosely in knit on WS.

Neckband

With RS facing and beg at center front, pick up and knit sts around neck edge.	**65**	**68**	**70**	**72**

Knit 2 rows.

Bind off loosely in knit on WS.

Button Band *(left front for girls; right front for boys)*

With RS facing, pick up and knit sts evenly spaced along front edge (approx 3 sts for every 4 rows).	**48**	**48**	**52**	**52**

Knit 6 rows.

Bind off loosely in knit on WS.

Buttonhole Band

With RS facing, pick up and knit the same number of sts as for button band.

For Girls

Rows 1 and 2: Knit.

Row 3 (Buttonhole row, WS): K2, ssk, yo twice, k2tog, [k , ssk, yo twice, k2tog] 4 times, k2—5 buttonholes made.	**6**	**6**	**7**	**7**

Rows 4–7: Knit.

Bind off loosely in knit on WS.

For Boys

Rows 1–3: Knit.

Row 4 (Buttonhole row, RS): K2, ssk, yo twice, k2tog, [k , ssk, yo twice, k2tog] 4 times, k2—5 buttonholes made.	**6**	**6**	**7**	**7**

Rows 5–6: Knit. RS row.

Bind off loosely in knit on WS.

Finishing

Weave in ends.

Block lightly to open up lace.

Using matching sewing thread, sew on buttons and backer buttons.

Ready for that special little one! •

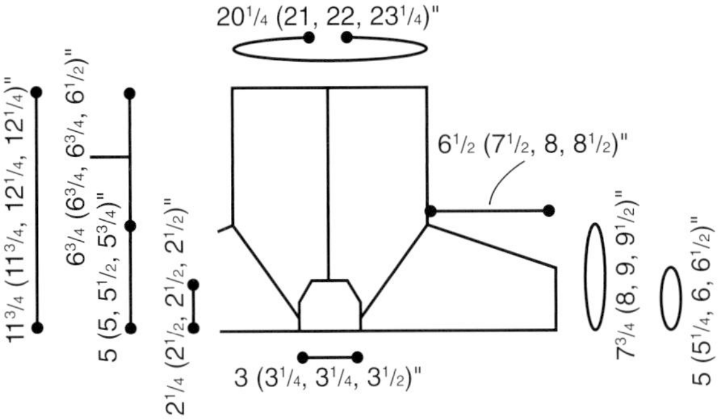

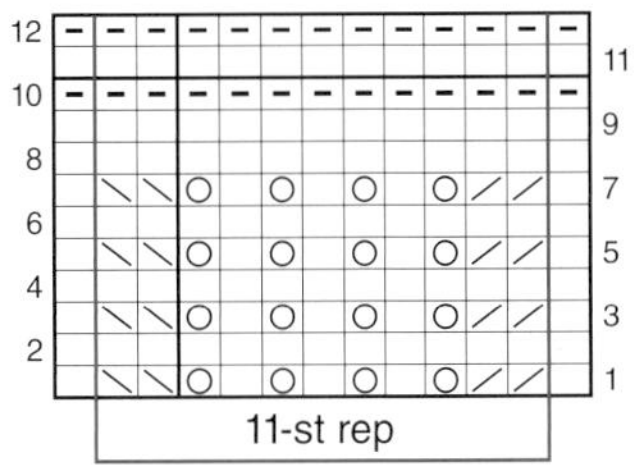

CREST OF THE WAVE

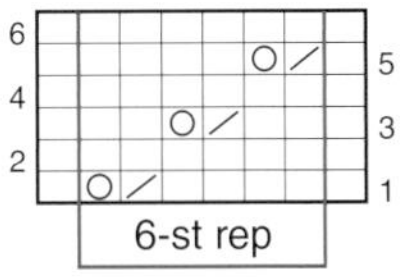

EYELETS CHART

STITCH KEY

- □ K on RS, p on WS
- ▭ P on RS, k on WS
- ⁄ K2tog
- \ Ssk
- ○ Yo

Diamonds & Lace

This top-down cardigan with optional waist shaping is lovely lace for any lady!

Skill level
Intermediate

Sizes
Women's sizes with standard fit

Finished Measurements
Chest (buttoned): inches
Length: inches

	Small 32–34	Medium 36–38	Large 40–42	X-Large 44–46	2X-Large 48–50	3X-Large 52–54
Chest (buttoned) (inches)	37	41	45	49	53	57
Length (inches)	23	23	24	24	25	25
Balls garnet mix #355	12	13	15	17	19	21

Materials
- Plymouth Encore DK (DK weight; 75% acrylic/25% wool; 150 yds/50g per ball): balls garnet mix #355 (3 LIGHT)
- Size 6 (4mm) 40-inch circular needle or size needed to obtain gauge
- Stitch markers in 2 colors
- 6 (1-inch) buttons #92425 from JHB International
- 6 (5/8-inch) backer buttons #40802 from JHB International
- Piece of smooth, lightweight scrap yarn about 5 inches long in a contrasting color
- Sewing needle and thread to match sweater color

Gauge
22 sts and 28 rows = 4 inches/10cm in St st.
To save time, take time to check gauge.

Special Abbreviations
Make 1 (M1): Insert LH needle from front to back under the designated running thread between sts; knit into the back of resulting loop.
Double yarn over (2yo): [Yo] twice. On next row, work (k1, p1) into 2yo.

Slip marker (sm): Slip marker from LH to RH needle.

Pattern Stitch

Note: A chart is provided for those preferring to work pat st from a chart.

Lace (multiple of 12 sts)

Row 1 (RS): *K5, k2tog, yo, k5; rep from * across.

Row 2 and all WS rows: Purl.

Row 3: *K4, [k2tog, yo] twice, k4; rep from * across.

Row 5: *K3, [k2tog, yo] 3 times, k3; rep from * across.

Row 7: *K2, [k2tog, yo] 4 times, k2; rep from * across.

Row 9: *K1, [k2tog, yo] 5 times, k1; rep from * across.

Row 11: *K2, [k2tog, yo] 4 times, k2; rep from * across.

Row 13: *K3, [k2tog, yo] 3 times, k3; rep from * across.

Row 15: *K4, [k2tog, yo] twice, k4; rep from * across.

Row 16: Purl.

Rep Rows 1–16 for pat.

Patten Note

Before beginning, be sure to read the Before You Get Started section for complete information on top-down architecture, seaming techniques, size selection and more.

Yoke

Cast on sts.	**44**	**49**	**52**	**53**	**58**	**60**
Set-up row (WS): P right front sts, pm;	**2**	**3**	**2**	**2**	**3**	**3**
p right sleeve sts, pm;	**6**	**6**	**6**	**6**	**6**	**6**
p back sts, pm;	**28**	**31**	**36**	**37**	**40**	**42**
p left sleeve sts, pm;	**6**	**6**	**6**	**6**	**6**	**6**
p left front sts.	**2**	**3**	**2**	**2**	**3**	**3**
Row 1 (RS): [Knit to 1 st before marker, yo, k1, sm, k1, yo] 4 times, knit to end. ***Note:** Each completed Row 1 adds 8 sts.*						
sts	**52**	**57**	**60**	**61**	**66**	**68**

Row 2: Purl.						
Rep Rows 1 and 2 more times.	5	5	4	5	5	5
sts	92	97	92	101	106	108

Shape Front Neck Edge

Row 3 (RS): Kfb, [knit to 1 st before marker, yo, k1, sm, k1, yo] 4 times, knit to last 2 sts, kfb, k1. *Note: Each completed Row 3 adds 10 sts.*						
sts	102	107	102	111	116	118
Row 4: Purl.						
Rep Rows 3 and 4 more times.	4	4	5	6	6	6
sts	142	147	152	171	176	178
Next row (RS): Cast on sts, [knit to 1 st before marker, k1, yo, sm, yo, k1] 4 times, knit to end.	3	4	6	6	6	6
sts	153	159	166	185	190	192
Next row (WS): Cast on sts, purl to end. *Note: The neck edge shaping is now complete.*	3	4	6	6	6	6
sts	156	163	172	191	196	198
Work Rows 1 and 2 more times.	14	18	22	18	19	20
sts	268	307	348	335	348	358
Row 5: [Knit to 1 st before marker, k1, yo, sm, k1, yo, ssk, knit to 3 sts before next marker, k2tog, yo, k1, sm, k1, yo] twice, knit to end. *Note: Each completed Row 5 inc fronts and back only, adding 4 sts.*						
sts	272	311	352	339	352	362
Row 6: Purl.						
Work Rows 5 and 6 more times.	4	2	0	4	5	6
sts	288	319	352	355	372	386
Row 7: [Knit to 2 sts before marker, M1, k1, yo, k1, sm, k1, yo, ssk, knit to 3 sts before next marker, k2tog, yo, k1, sm, k1, yo, k1, M1] twice, knit to end. *Note: Each completed Row 7 inc fronts and back only, adding 8 sts.*						
sts	296	327	360	363	380	394
Work 2 rows even, or until center back measures at least inches from cast-on edge, ending with a RS row.	9½	10	10½	11	11½	12
sts each front	43	47	51	54	57	59
sts each sleeve	58	66	74	70	72	74
back sts	94	101	110	115	122	128

Divide for Right Sleeve

With WS facing, purl across right front to first marker and right sleeve to 2nd marker; remove this marker and turn.

Right Sleeve

Row 1 (RS): Cast on ___ sts and knit to marker, adding a boundary line near center of sleeve; remove this marker and turn.	4	5	6	9	11	14
Row 2: Cast on ___ sts and purl across sleeve.	4	5	6	9	11	14
___ sleeve sts	66	76	86	88	94	102
Option 1: Standard Sleeve Length: ___ inches to underarm	17	17	17½	17½	18	18
Work sleeve even until sleeve measures ___ inch from boundary line, ending with a WS row.	1	1	½	½	½	¼
Dec row (RS): K1, k2tog, knit to last 3 sts, ssk, k1. ___ sts	64	74	84	86	92	100
*Work ___ inch even, ending with a WS row; work Dec row.	¾	½	½	½	½	½
Rep from * ___ more times.	18	22	26	26	28	31
___ sts	28	30	32	34	36	38
At the same time, when sleeve measures ___ inches from boundary line, or 4 inches less than desired length, ending with a RS row, count the number of sleeve sts.	13	13	13½	13½	14	14

___ sts

Divide by 2: ___ sts

Subtract 6: ___ sts = S

Set-up row (WS): P ___ (S) sts, pm, p12, pm, purl to end.

Next row (RS): Knit to marker, work Lace pat between markers, knit to end.

Continue shaping sleeve; work 16 more rows of Lace pat between markers, ending with Row 1. When Lace pat is complete, remove markers and continue in St st.

After shaping is complete, work even until sleeve measures ___ inches from boundary line or 1½ inches less than desired length, ending with a WS row.	15½	15½	16	16	16½	16½

Dec row (RS): Knit and dec ____ st(s) evenly spaced across row.	0	0	1	1	1	1
____ sts	28	30	31	33	35	37

Knit 8 rows.

Bind off loosely in knit on WS.

Cut yarn, leaving a long tail. Use tail to sew sleeve seam using mattress st.

Option 2: Custom Sleeve Length

Your measurement from wrist to underarm: ____ inches

Subtract 2 inches = A ____

____ number of dec = B	19	23	27	27	29	32

Divide A by (B + 1) = ____ how far between dec in inches = C

Work sleeve even until sleeve measures ____ inch (C) from boundary line, ending with a WS row.

Dec row (RS): K1, k2tog, knit to last 3 sts, ssk, k1. ____ sts	64	74	84	86	92	100
*Work ____ inch (C) even, ending after a WS row; work Dec row; rep from * ____ more times.	17	21	25	25	27	30
____ sts	28	30	32	34	36	38

At the same time, when sleeve measures 4 inches less than desired length from boundary line, ending with a RS row, count the number of sts in sleeve.

____ sts

Divide by 2: ____ sts

Subtract 6: ____ sts = S

Next row (RS): Knit to marker, work Lace pat between markers, knit to end.

Continue shaping sleeve; work 16 more rows of Lace pat between markers, ending with Row 1. When Lace pat is complete, remove markers and continue in St st.

After shaping is complete, work even until sleeve measures 1½ inches less than desired length from boundary line, ending with a WS row.

Dec row (RS): Knit and dec ____ st(s) evenly spaced across row.	0	0	1	1	1	1
____ sts	28	30	31	33	35	37

Knit 8 rows.

Bind off loosely in knit on WS.

Cut yarn, leaving a long tail. Use tail to sew sleeve seam using mattress st.

Divide for Left Sleeve

With WS facing, attach yarn adjacent to base of completed right sleeve. Purl across back to first marker and left sleeve to 2nd marker; remove this marker and turn.

Left Sleeve *(both options)*

Work as for right sleeve.

Body

With WS facing, attach yarn to back of sweater adjacent to base of completed left sleeve. Purl across left front.

Unification row (RS): Knit across left front sts; *M1 using loose strand between previous section and sleeve, pick up and knit sts across underarm of sleeve to seam, pm for side, pick up and knit sts across rest of sleeve underarm, M1 using loose strand between sleeve and next section;** knit across back sts; rep from * to ** at base of right sleeve; knit across right front sts.

sts

Next row: Using different-color markers, mark positions for Lace pat as follows: p2, pm,
p , pm, purl to side marker;
p , pm,
p , pm, purl to side marker;
p , pm,
p , pm, p2.

43	47	51	54	57	59
3	5	6	9	11	14
3	5	6	9	11	14
94	101	110	115	122	128
43	47	51	54	57	59
196	219	240	263	284	306
36	36	48	48	60	60
9	9	8	8	13	13
84	96	108	120	120	132
9	15	8	14	7	12
36	36	48	48	60	60

Option 1: Lace Body Without Waist Shaping

Work even until back measures inches from cast-on edge at center back, ending with a WS row.

14	14	15	15	16	16

Next row (RS): Slipping side markers, k2, [work Lace pat to next marker, knit to next lace marker] twice, work Lace pat to next marker, k2.

Working Lace pat between markers and St st outside markers, complete 3 16-row reps of Lace pat, then work Row 1 once more.						
Work even in St st until back measures inches from cast-on edge at center back, or 1½ inches less than desired length, ending with a WS row.	**21½**	**21½**	**22½**	**22½**	**23½**	**23½**
Dec row (RS): Knit and dec sts evenly spaced across row.	**20**	**22**	**24**	**26**	**28**	**31**
sts	**176**	**197**	**216**	**237**	**256**	**275**
Knit 12 rows, ending with a RS row.						
Bind off loosely in knit on WS.						
Option 2: Lace Body With Waist Shaping						
Work as for Option 1, setting up and working Lace pat in same manner, and *at the same time*, shape waist as follows:						
Work even until back measures inches from cast-on edge at center back, ending with a WS row.	**14**	**14**	**14½**	**14½**	**15**	**15**
Dec row (RS): [Work to 2 sts before side marker, k2tog, sm, ssk] twice, work to end. ***Note:** Every completed Dec row removes 4 sts.*						
sts	**200**	**220**	**244**	**265**	**288**	**312**
Rep Dec row every 2 inches twice more.						
sts	**192**	**212**	**236**	**257**	**280**	**304**
Work 1 inch even, ending after a WS row.						
Inc row (RS): [Work to 1 st before marker, kfb, sm, kfb] twice, work to end. ***Note:** Every completed Inc row adds 4 sts.*						
sts	**196**	**216**	**240**	**261**	**284**	**308**
Rep Inc row every inch twice more.						
sts	**204**	**224**	**248**	**269**	**292**	**316**
Work even until back measures inches from cast-on edge at center back, or 1½ inches less than desired length, ending with a WS row.	**21½**	**21½**	**22½**	**22½**	**23½**	**23½**
Dec row (RS): Knit and dec sts evenly spaced across row.	**20**	**22**	**25**	**27**	**29**	**32**
sts	**184**	**202**	**223**	**242**	**263**	**284**
Knit 12 rows.						
Bind off loosely in knit on WS.						

Neckband

With RS facing, beg at center front and using smaller needle, pick up and knit sts around neck edge.

84 85 92 92 100 104

Knit 10 rows.

Bind off loosely in knit on WS.

Button Band

With RS facing, pick up and knit sts evenly spaced along left front edge (approx 3 sts for every 4 rows).

107 107 112 112 117 117

Knit 12 rows.

Bind off loosely in knit on WS.

Buttonhole Band

With RS facing, pick up and knit the same number of sts as for button band.

Rows 1–6: Knit.

Row 7 (Buttonhole row, WS): K3, ssk, 2yo, k2tog, [k , ssk, 2yo, k2tog] 5 times, knit to end—6 buttonholes made.

15 15 16 16 17 17

Row 8: Knit across, working (k1, p1) in 2yos.

Rows 9–12: Knit.

Bind off loosely in knit on WS.

Finishing

Weave in ends. Block to open up lace.

Using matching sewing thread, sew on buttons and backer buttons.

Wear it with diamonds—or jeans! •

STITCH KEY

- ☐ K on RS, p on WS
- ⧄ K2tog
- ⊡ Yo

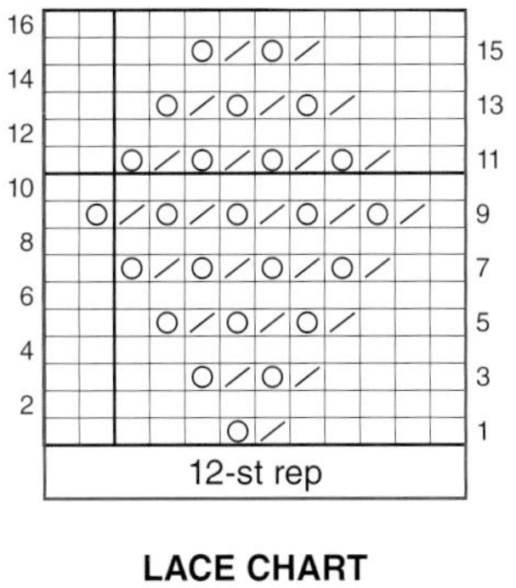

LACE CHART

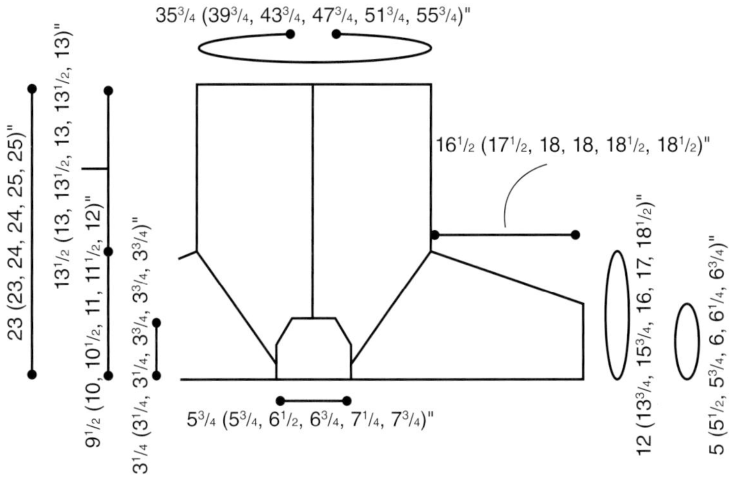

Baby's First Fair Isle

Whether you make the hearts and flowers pattern or the fun diagonal stripes, your special baby will look very stylish in this Fair Isle cardi.

Skill level

Intermediate

Sizes

Baby with standard fit	6 mo	12 mo	18 mo	24 mo
Finished Measurements				
Chest (buttoned): inches	21	21¾	22¾	24
Length: inches	11¾	11¾	12¼	12¼

Materials

- Cascade 220 Sport (sport weight; 100% wool; 164 yds/50g per skein):
- For Girl's sweater (shown on model):

	6 mo	12 mo	18 mo	24 mo
skeins natural #8010 (MC)	2	3	4	4
skein cotton candy #9478 (CC1),	1	1	1	1
skein purple hyacinth #7808 (CC2)	1	1	1	1
skein cerise #7802 (CC3)	1	1	1	1

- For Boy's sweater (shown on swatch):

	6 mo	12 mo	18 mo	24 mo
skeins azure #8892 (MC)	2	3	4	4
skein beige #8021 (CC)	1	1	1	1

- Size 4 (3.5mm) 32-inch circular needle or 2 sizes smaller than needle used for body
- Size 6 (4mm) 32-inch circular needle or size needed to obtain gauge
- Stitch markers
- 5 (½-inch) buttons #90890 from JHB International
- 5 (½-inch) backer buttons #40800 from JHB International
- Piece of smooth, lightweight scrap yarn about 5 inches long in a contrasting color
- Sewing thread to match main color

Gauge
22 sts and 28 rows = 4 inches/10cm in 1- and 2-color St st with larger needle.
To save time, take time to check gauge.

Special Abbreviations
Make 1 (M1): Insert LH needle from front to back under the designated running thread between sts; knit into the back of resulting loop.
Decrease in Rib (rib2tog): K2tog or p2tog as needed to maintain the established rib pat.
Slip marker (sm): Slip marker from RH to LH needle.

Pattern Stitches
Girl's Color pat (multiple of 10 sts + 2, *shown on model*)
See chart.

Boy's Color pat (multiple of 4 sts + 4, *shown on swatch*)
See chart.

2x2 Rib (multiple of 4 sts + 2)
Row 1 (WS): P2, *k2, p2; rep from * to end.
Row 2 (RS): K2, *p2, p2; rep from * to end.
Rep Rows 1 and 2 for pat.

Pattern Note
Before beginning, be sure to read the Before You Get Started section for complete information on top-down architecture, seaming techniques, size selection and more.

Tip

Stitch gauge is critical, row gauge is less so. Check your gauge in both St st and color pattern. Many knitters find it necessary to go up at least 1 needle size to maintain gauge while knitting stranded 2-color stockinette stitch.

Yoke

With larger needle and MC, cast on sts.	**31**	**34**	**36**	**38**
Set-up row (WS): P right front sts, pm,	**2**	**2**	**2**	**2**
p right sleeve sts, pm,	**5**	**6**	**7**	**8**
p back sts, pm,	**17**	**18**	**18**	**18**
p left sleeve sts, pm,	**5**	**6**	**7**	**8**
p left front sts.	**2**	**2**	**2**	**2**
Row 1 (RS): [Knit to 1 st before marker, kfb, sm, kfb] 4 times, knit to end. ***Note:*** *Each completed Row 1 adds 8 sts.*				
sts	**39**	**42**	**44**	**46**
Row 2: Purl.				
Rep [Rows 1 and 2] more times.	**2**	**2**	**2**	**2**
sts	**55**	**58**	**60**	**62**

Shape Front Neck Edge

Row 3 (RS): Kfb, [knit to 1 st before marker, kfb, sm, kfb] 4 times knit to last 2 sts, kfb, k1. ***Note:*** *Each completed Row 3 adds 10 sts.*				
sts	**65**	**68**	**70**	**72**
Row 4: Purl.				
Rep Rows 3 and 4 more times.	**3**	**4**	**4**	**4**
sts	**95**	**108**	**110**	**112**
Next row (RS): Cast on 4 sts, [knit to 1 st before marker, kfb, sm, kfb] 4 times, knit to end.				
sts	**107**	**120**	**122**	**124**
Next row (WS): Cast on 4 sts, purl to end.				
sts	**111**	**124**	**126**	**128**
The neck edge shaping is now complete.				
Work Rows 1 and 2 more times.	**8**	**7**	**9**	**10**
total sts	**175**	**180**	**198**	**208**
Work 1 row even or until center back measures at least inches from cast-on edge, ending with a RS row.	**5**	**5**	**5½**	**5¾**
sts each front	**26**	**27**	**29**	**30**
sts each sleeve	**37**	**38**	**43**	**46**
back sts	**49**	**50**	**54**	**56**

Divide for Right Sleeve

With WS facing, purl across right front to first marker and right sleeve to 2nd marker; remove this marker and turn.

Right Sleeve

Row 1 (RS): Cast on 3 sts; knit to marker, adding a boundary line near center of sleeve; remove this marker and turn.				
sts	**40**	**41**	**46**	**49**

Row 2: Cast on 3 sts; purl across sleeve sts.				
sleeve sts	43	44	49	52
Work sleeve even until sleeve measures inch(es) from boundary line, ending with a WS row.	¾	1	1½	1¾
Dec row (RS): K1, k2tog, knit to last 3 sts, ssk, k1.				
sts	41	42	47	50
[Work ¾ inch even inch, ending with a WS row; work Dec row] 5 times.				
sts	31	32	37	40
Work even until sleeve measures inches from boundary line or ¾ inch less than desired length, ending with a WS row.	5¾	6¾	7¼	7¾
Dec row (RS): Knit and dec st(s) evenly spaced across row.	1	2	3	2
sts	30	30	34	38

Change to smaller needle; work ¾ inch in 2x2 Rib.

Bind off loosely in rib.

Cut yarn, leaving a long tail. Use this tail to sew sleeve seam using mattress st.

Tip

To ensure a loose bind-off, hold the larger needle in your right hand while binding off.

Divide for Left Sleeve

With WS facing, attach MC to sweater back adjacent to base of completed right sleeve. Purl across back sts to first marker and left sleeve sts to 2nd marker; remove this marker and turn.

Left Sleeve

Work as for right sleeve.

Body

With WS facing, attach MC adjacent to base of completed left sleeve. Purl across left front sts.

Unification row (RS): Knit across left front sts,	26	27	29	30
*M1 using loose strand between previous section and sleeve, pick up and knit 4 sts across sleeve underarm, M1 using loose strand between sleeve and next section;** knit across				
back sts;	49	50	54	56
rep from * to **; knit across right front sts.	26	27	29	30
sts	113	116	124	128
Work even until back measures inches from cast-on edge at center back, ending with a WS row.	7½	7½	8	8
Next row (RS): Knit and st(s) evenly spaced across.	Dec 1	Dec 4	Dec 2	Inc 4
sts	112	112	122	132

Beg color pat of choice.

For Girl's pat: Work Rows 1–24 of chart, then continue with MC only.

For Boy's pat: Rep [Rows 1–8] 3 times, then continue with MC only.

Work even until back measures inches from cast-on edge at center back or ¾ inch less than desired length, ending with a RS row. — 11 | 11 | 11½ | 11½

Dec row (RS): With MC, knit and dec sts evenly spaced across row. — 10 | 10 | 12 | 14

sts — 102 | 102 | 110 | 118

Change to smaller needle and work in 2x2 Rib for ¾ inch.

Bind off loosely in rib.

Neckband

With RS facing and beg at center front, using smaller needle and MC, pick up and knit sts around neck edge. — 66 | 66 | 70 | 70

Work 4 rows in 2x2 Rib, ending with a RS row.

Bind off loosely in knit on WS.

Button Band *(left front for girls; right front for boys)*

With RS facing and using smaller needle and MC, pick up and knit sts evenly spaced along front edge (approx 3 sts for every 4 rows). — 50 | 50 | 58 | 58

Work 6 rows in 2x2 Rib.

Bind off loosely in rib.

Buttonhole Band

With RS facing and using smaller needle and MC, pick up and knit the same number of sts as for button band.

For Girls

Rows 1 and 2: Work in 2x2 Rib.

Row 3 (Buttonhole row, WS): Work 5 sts in rib, rib2tog, yo, [work sts, rib2tog, yo] 4 times, work 3 sts to end—5 buttonholes made. — 8 | 8 | 10 | 10

Rows 4–6: Work in established rib.

Bind off loosely in knit on WS.

For Boys

Rows 1–3: Work in 2x2 Rib.

Row 4 (Buttonhole row, RS): Work 5 sts in rib, rib2tog, yo, [work sts, rib2tog, yo] 4 times, work to end—5 buttonholes made. — 8 | 8 | 10 | 10

Rows 5 and 6: Work in established rib.

Bind off loosely in knit on WS.

Finishing

Weave in ends. Block lightly.

Using matching sewing thread, sew on buttons and backer buttons.

What a cutie! •

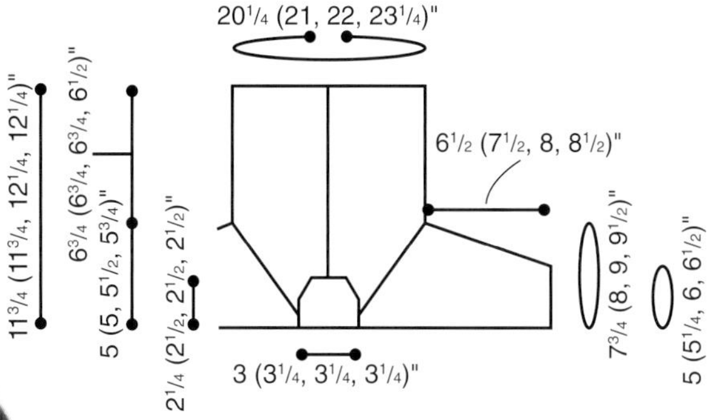

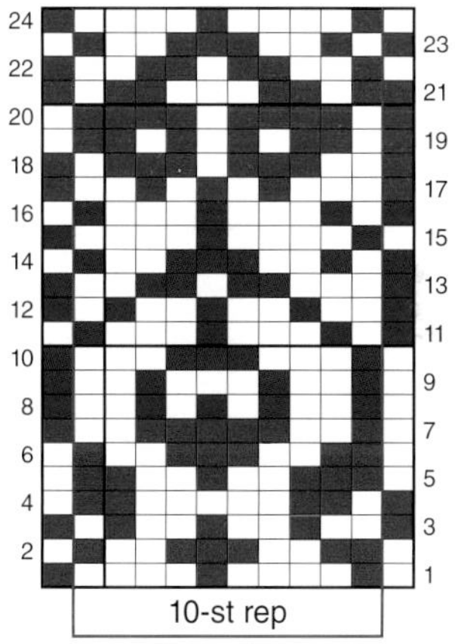

GIRL'S COLOR CHART

COLOR KEY
MC
CC1
CC2
CC3

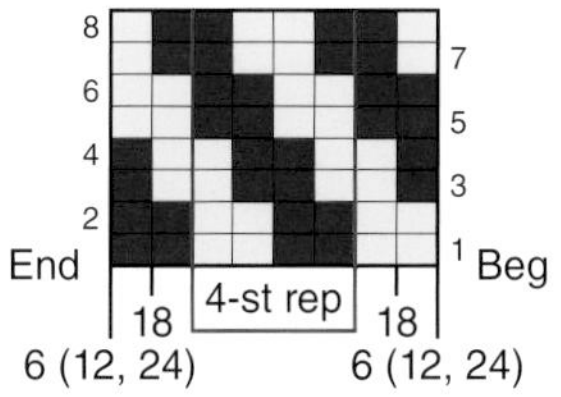

BOY'S COLOR CHART

COLOR KEY
MC
CC

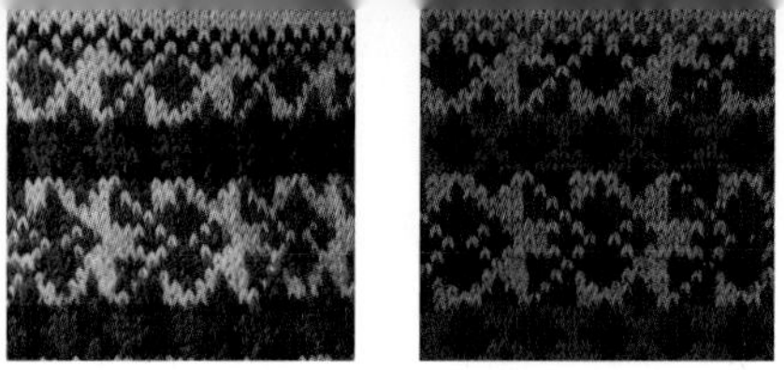

Sweet Clover

This sweater is the perfect vehicle to express your love of color.

Skill Level

Intermediate

Sizes

Adult with standard fit

	Small	Medium	Large	X-Large	2X-Large	3X-Large
	32–34	36–38	40–42	44–46	48–50	52–54

Finished Measurements

	Small	Medium	Large	X-Large	2X-Large	3X-Large
Chest (buttoned): inches	37	41	45	49	53	57
Length: inches	23	24	25	26	26	26

Materials

- Cascade 220 Heathers (worsted weight; 100% wool; 220 yds/100g per skein): (4 MEDIUM)

	Small	Medium	Large	X-Large	2X-Large	3X-Large
Colorway 1 (shown on model)						
skeins rose quartz heather #9575 (MC)	6	8	9	10	11	12
skeins satine #2434 (CC1)	2	2	2	2	2	2
skein merlot heather #9443 (CC2)	1	1	1	1	1	1
Colorway 2 (shown on swatch)						
skeins straw #4010 (MC)	6	8	9	10	11	12
skeins mocha heather #9446 (CC1)	2	2	2	2	2	2
skein Provence #2425 (CC2)	1	1	1	1	1	1

- Size 5 (3.75mm) 32-inch circular needle or 2 sizes smaller than needle used for body
- Size 7 (4.5mm) 40-inch circular needle or size needed to obtain gauge
- 6 (1-inch) buttons #90523 from JHB International
- 6 (⅝-inch) backer buttons #40802 from JHB International
- Stitch markers
- Piece of smooth, lightweight scrap yarn about 5 inches long in a contrasting color
- Sewing thread to match main color

Gauge

20 sts and 27 rows = 4 inches/10cm in 1-color and 2-color St st with larger needle.

To save time, take time to check gauge.

Tip

Stitch gauge is critical, row gauge is less so. Check your gauge in both St st and color pattern. Many knitters find it necessary to go up at least 1 needle size to maintain gauge while knitting stranded 2-color stockinette stitch.

Special Abbreviations

Make 1 (M1): Insert LH needle from front to back under the designated running thread between sts; knit into the back of resulting loop.

Slip marker (sm): Slip marker from LH to RH needle.

Pattern Stitches

Border Pat (even number of sts)
See Chart A.

Body Pat (multiple of 12 sts + 2)
See Chart B.

2x2 Rib (multiple of 4 sts + 2)
Row 1 (WS): P2, *k2, p2; rep from * to end.
Row 2 (RS): K2, *p2, k1; rep from * to end.
Rep Rows 1 and 2 for pat.

Pattern Note

Before beginning, be sure to read the Before You Get Started section for complete information on top-down architecture, seaming techniques, size selection and more.

Yoke

Using larger needle and MC, cast on sts.	**39**	**43**	**45**	**49**	**53**	**59**
Set-up row (WS): P right front sts, pm,	**2**	**2**	**2**	**2**	**2**	**3**
p right sleeve sts, pm,	**5**	**5**	**5**	**5**	**5**	**7**
p back sts, pm,	**25**	**29**	**31**	**35**	**39**	**39**
p left sleeve sts, pm,	**5**	**5**	**5**	**5**	**5**	**7**
p left front sts.	**2**	**2**	**2**	**2**	**2**	**3**
Row 1 (RS): [Knit to 1 st before marker, kfb, sm, kfb] 4 times, knit to end. ***Note:** Each completed Row 1 adds 8 sts.*						
sts	**47**	**51**	**53**	**57**	**61**	**67**
Row 2: Purl.						
Rep Rows 1 and 2 more times.	**6**	**6**	**6**	**4**	**6**	**5**
sts	**95**	**99**	**101**	**89**	**109**	**107**

Shape Front Neck Edge						
Row 3 (RS): Kfb, [knit to 1 st before marker, kfb, sm, kfb] 4 times, knit to last 2 sts, kfb, k1. *Note: Each completed Row 3 adds 10 sts.*						
sts	105	109	111	99	119	117
Row 4: Purl.						
Rep Rows 3 and 4 more times.	3	3	4	6	6	7
sts	135	139	151	159	179	187
Next row (RS): Cast on sts, [knit to 1 st before marker, kfb, sm, kfb] 4 times, knit to end.	3	7	5	5	5	5
sts	146	152	164	172	192	200
Next row (WS): Cast on sts, purl to end. The neck shaping is now complete.	3	5	5	5	5	5
sts	149	157	169	177	197	205
Work Rows 1 and 2 more times.	11	14	17	18	16	24
sts	237	269	305	321	325	381
Row 5: [Knit to 1 st before marker, kfb, sm, knit to next marker, sm, kfb] twice, knit to end. *Note: Each completed Row 5 inc fronts and back only, adding 4 sts.*						
sts	247	275	311	319	322	381
Row 6: Purl.						
Work Rows 5 and 6 more time(s).	7	5	4	4	6	1
sts	265	289	321	337	349	389
Work 1 row even or until center back measures at least inches from cast-on edge, ending with a RS row.	9½	10	10½	11	11½	12
sts each front	39	42	46	49	51	55
sts each sleeve	51	57	65	67	67	81
back sts	85	91	99	105	113	117

Divide for Right Sleeve

Purl across right front sts to first marker and right sleeve sts to 2nd marker; remove this marker and turn.

Right Sleeve						
Row 1 (RS): *Cast on sts and knit to marker, adding a boundary line near center of sleeve; remove this marker and turn.	4	5	6	8	10	12
Row 2: Cast on sts; purl across sleeve.	4	5	6	8	10	12
sleeve sts	59	67	77	83	87	105

Option 1: Standard Sleeve Length: inches to underarm	**16½**	**17½**	**18**	**18**	**18½**	**18½**
Work even until sleeve measures inch(es) from boundary line, ending with a WS row.	**1½**	**1**	**¾**	**1½**	**1½**	**½**
Dec row (RS): K1, k2tog, knit to last 3 sts, ssk, k1.						
sts	**57**	**65**	**75**	**81**	**85**	**103**
*Work inch even, ending after a WS	**¾**	**¾**	**¾**	**½**	**½**	**½**
row; work Dec row; rep from * more times.	**13**	**16**	**20**	**21**	**22**	**30**
sts	**31**	**33**	**35**	**39**	**41**	**43**
At the same time, when sleeve measures inches from boundary line, or 3½ inches less than desired length, ending after a WS row, work 6-row Border pat, then continue with MC only.	**12½**	**13½**	**14**	**14**	**14½**	**14½**
After shaping is complete, work even until sleeve measures inches from boundary line or 2 inches less than desired length, ending with a WS row.	**14½**	**15½**	**16**	**16**	**16½**	**16½**
Dec row (RS): Knit and dec st(s) evenly spaced across row.	**1**	**3**	**1**	**1**	**3**	**1**
sts	**30**	**30**	**34**	**38**	**38**	**42**
Change to smaller needle; work 2x2 Rib for 2 inches.						
Bind off loosely in rib.						
Cut yarn, leaving a long tail. Cut yarn, leaving a long tail. Use this tail to sew sleeve seam using mattress st.						
Option 2: Custom Sleeve Length						
Your measurement from wrist to underarm: inches						
Subtract 2 inches = A						
number of dec = B	**14**	**17**	**21**	**22**	**23**	**31**
Divide A by (B + 1) = how far between dec in inches = C						
Work even until sleeve measures inches (C) from boundary line, ending with a WS row.						
Dec row (RS): K1, k2tog, knit to last 3 sts, ssk, k1.						
sts	**57**	**65**	**75**	**81**	**85**	**103**
*Work even for inch (C), ending with a WS row; work Dec row; rep from * more times.	**13**	**16**	**20**	**21**	**22**	**30**
sts	**31**	**33**	**35**	**39**	**41**	**43**

At the same time, when sleeve measures 3½ inches less than desired length, ending after a WS row, work 6-row Border pat, then continue with MC only.

After shaping is complete, work even until sleeve measures inches (A) from boundary line or 2 inches less than desired length, ending after a WS row.

Dec row (RS): Knit and dec st(s) evenly spaced across row.

sts

Dec	**1**	**3**	**1**	**1**	**3**	**1**
sts	**30**	**30**	**34**	**38**	**38**	**42**

Change to smaller needle and work 2x2 Rib for 2 inches.

Bind off loosely in rib.

Cut yarn, leaving a long tail. Cut yarn, leaving a long tail. Use this tail to sew sleeve seam using mattress st.

Divide for Left Sleeve *(both options)*

With WS facing, attach yarn adjacent to base of completed right sleeve. Purl across back sts to first marker and left sleeve sts to 2nd marker; remove this marker and turn.

Left Sleeve

Work as for right sleeve.

Body

With WS facing, attach yarn adjacent to base of completed left sleeve. Purl across left front sts.

Unification row (RS): Knit across left front sts, *M1 using loose strand between previous section and sleeve, pick up and knit sts across underarm of sleeve to seam, pm, pick up and knit sts across rest of sleeve underarm, M1 using loose strand between sleeve and next section**, knit across back sts, rep from * to ** at base of right sleeve, knit across right front.

sts

Work even until back measures inches from cast-on edge at center back, ending with a RS row.

left front sts	**39**	**42**	**46**	**49**	**51**	**55**
sts across underarm to seam	**3**	**5**	**6**	**8**	**10**	**12**
sts across rest of underarm	**3**	**5**	**6**	**8**	**10**	**12**
back sts	**85**	**91**	**99**	**105**	**113**	**117**
sts	**179**	**199**	**219**	**239**	**259**	**279**
inches	**14¼**	**15¼**	**16¼**	**17¼**	**17¼**	**17¼**

	Inc 3	Dec 5	Dec 1	Inc 3	Dec 5	Dec 1
Next row (WS): Purl and st(s) evenly across row.	**Inc 3**	**Dec 5**	**Dec 1**	**Inc 3**	**Dec 5**	**Dec 1**
sts	**182**	**194**	**218**	**242**	**254**	**278**

Work 18-row Body chart, then rep Rows 3–18 until back measures inches from cast-on edge at center back, or 2 inches less than desired length, ending with a WS row.

inches	**21**	**22**	**23**	**24**	**24**	**24**

Change to smaller needle; with MC, work in 2x2 Rib for 2 inches.

Bind off loosely in rib.

Neckband

With RS facing, using smaller needle and MC, and beg at center front, pick up and knit sts around neck edge.

sts	**78**	**82**	**86**	**90**	**94**	**102**

Work 1 inch in 2x2 Rib.

Bind off loosely in rib.

Button Band *(left front for women; right front for men)*

With RS facing and using smaller needle and MC, pick up and knit sts evenly spaced along front edge (approx 3 sts for every 4 rows).

sts	**102**	**106**	**110**	**114**	**114**	**114**

Work 8 rows in 2x2 Rib. Bind off loosely in rib.

Buttonhole Band

With RS facing and using smaller needle and MC, pick up and knit the same number of sts as for button band.

For Women

Rows 1–4: Work in 2x2 Rib.

Row 5 (Buttonhole row, WS): Work 5 sts in rib, bind off 3 sts, [work sts in rib (including st on RH needle following bind-off), bind off 3 sts] 5 times, work to end—6 buttonholes made.

sts	**14**	**15**	**16**	**17**	**17**	**17**

Row 6: [Work to bound-off sts, cast on 3 sts] 6 times, work to end.

Rows 7–9: Work in established rib.

Bind off loosely in rib.

For Men

Rows 1–5: Work in 2x2 Rib.

Row 6 (Buttonhole row, RS): Work 5 sts in rib, bind off 3 sts, [work sts in rib (including st on RH needle following bind-off), bind off 3 sts] 5 times, work to end—6 buttonholes made.

14 15 16 17 17 17

Row 7: [Work to bound-off sts, cast on 3 sts] 6 times, work to end.

Rows 8 and 9: Work in established rib.

Bind off loosely in rib.

Finishing

Weave in ends. Block.

Using matching sewing thread, sew on buttons and backer buttons.

Congratulations! Isn't it beautiful? •

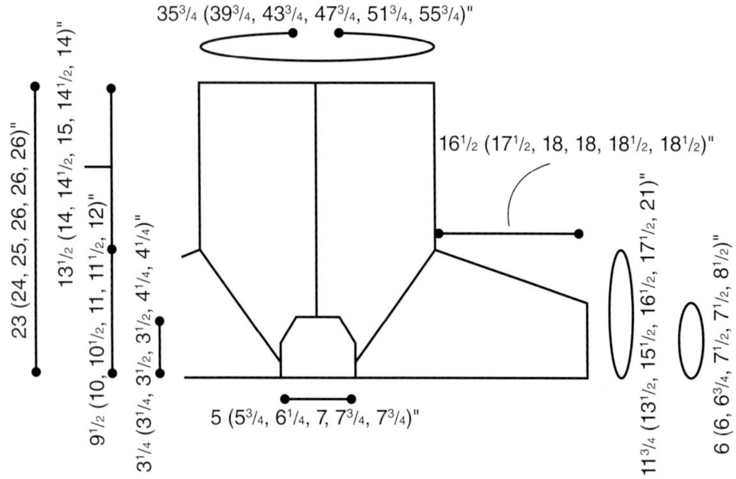

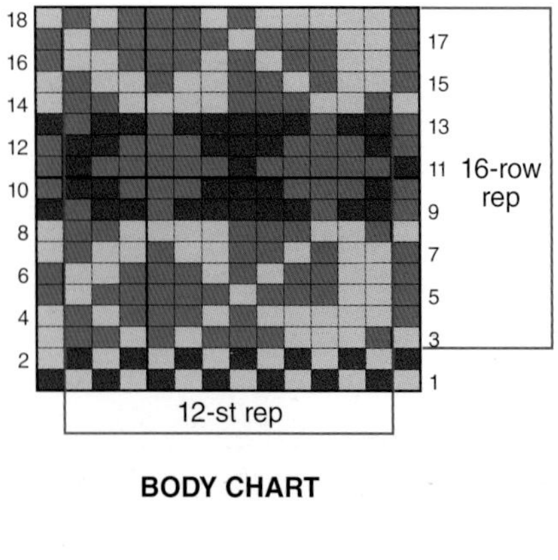

BODY CHART

COLOR KEY
MC
CC1
CC2

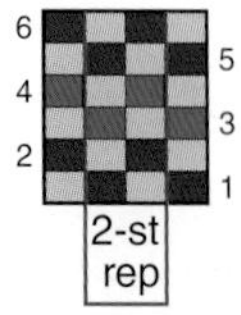

BORDER CHART

Knitting Basics

Cast-On Techniques

Knitted Cast-On

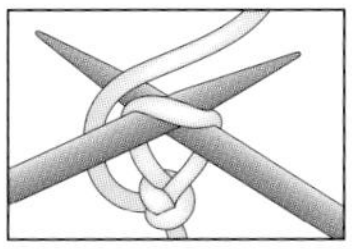

Make a slip knot on left needle. Insert tip of right needle into slip knot (loop). Knit 1 in loop. Place new stitch on left needle. Repeat until desired stitches are cast on.

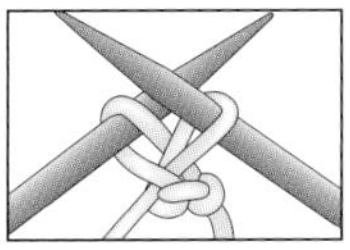

Cable Cast-On

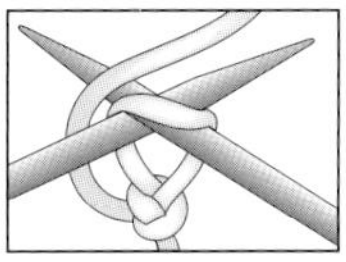

This type of cast-on is used when adding stitches in the middle or at the end of a row.

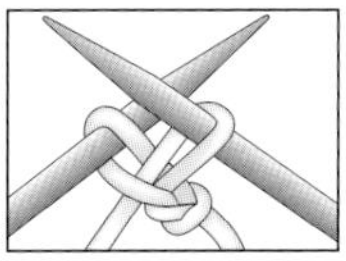

Make a slip knot on the left needle. Knit a stitch in this knot and place it on the left needle. Insert the right needle between the last two stitches on the left needle. Knit a stitch and place it on the left needle. Repeat for each stitch needed.

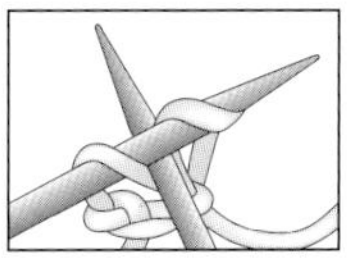

Decrease (Dec)

Knit 2 Together (K2tog)

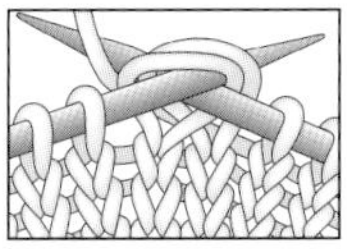

Put tip of right needle through next two stitches on left needle as to knit. Knit these two stitches as one.

Purl 2 Together (P2tog)

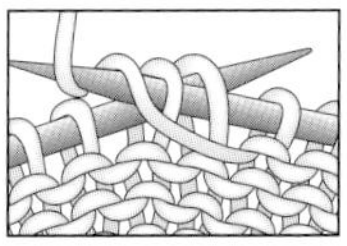

Put tip of right needle through next two stitches on left needle as to purl. Purl these two stitches as one.

Slip, Slip, Knit (Ssk)

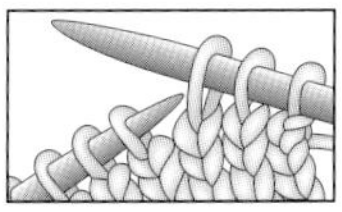

Slip next two stitches, one at a time as to knit, from left needle to right needle.

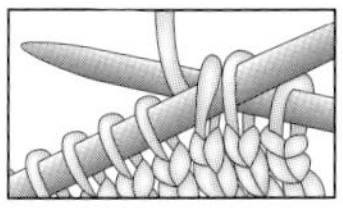

Insert left needle in front of both stitches and knit them together.

Pick Up & Knit

Step 1: With right side facing, working 1 st in from edge, insert tip of needle in space between first and second stitch.

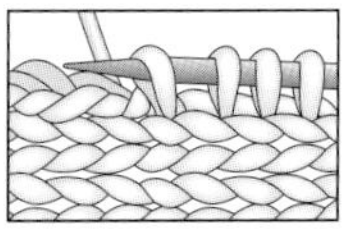

Step 2: Wrap yarn around needle.
Step 3: Pull loop through to front.
Step 4: Repeat Steps 1–3.

Increase (Inc)

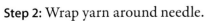

Knit Increase (kfb)

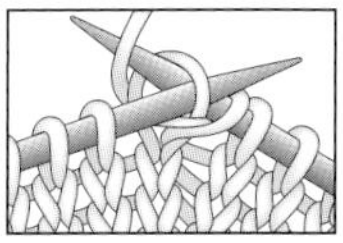

Knit the next stitch in the usual manner, but don't remove the stitch from the left needle. Place right needle behind left needle and knit again into the back of the same stitch.

Slip original stitch off left needle.

Make 1 With Left Twist (M1L)

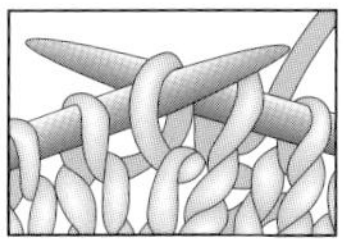

Insert left needle from front to back under the horizontal loop between the last stitch worked and next stitch on left needle.

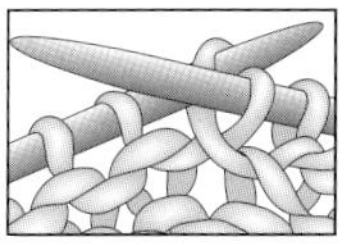

With right needle, knit into the back of this loop.

To make this increase on the purl side, insert left needle in same manner and purl into the back of the loop.

Mattress Stitch

To work this seam, thread a tapestry needle with matching yarn. Insert the needle into one corner of work from back to front, just above the cast-on stitch, leaving a 3-inch tail. Take needle to edge of other piece and bring it from back to front at the corner of this piece.

Return to the first piece and insert the needle from the right to wrong side where the thread comes out of the piece. Slip the needle upward under two horizontal threads and bring the needle through to the right side.

Cross to the other side and repeat the same process, going down where you came out, under two threads and up.

Continue working back and forth on the two pieces in the same manner for about an inch, then gently pull on the thread pulling the two pieces together.

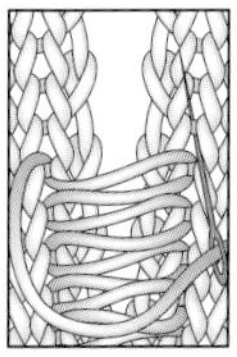

Complete the seam and fasten off.

Use the beginning tail to even-up the lower edge by working a figure-8 between the cast-on stitches at the corners. Insert the threaded needle from front to back under both threads of the corner cast-on stitch on the edge opposite the tail, then into the same stitch on the first edge. Pull gently until the "8" fills the gap.

Meet the Designer

Georgia Druen is the owner of HearthStone Knits the 2012 winner of the Best Yarn Shop in Saint Louis from *Riverfront Times*. Her personal fiber history began in childhood. Her mother taught her to both knit and crochet at such a young age, she can no longer recall how young she was—that means over 50 years of needle-arts experience! She is very grateful that her mom had a chance to see what those gifts of early lessons have meant. Today, life is a constant stream of knitting projects with moments stolen for crochet. Between knitting models for the shop and designing patterns for knitting magazines, it's hard to complete any personal knitting. For Georgia, the act of knitting soothes, the act of designing excites and the act of problem solving for customers inspires.

Acknowledgments

This project is truly a group effort. Many, many thanks to my wonderful friends and super test knitters, Sherry Duncan, Cilla Fleig, Laura Helton, Mandy Pedigo and Wendy West; to my editor, Kara Gott Warner, for entrusting me with this project; and to my family, especially my husband, for unflagging support and infinite patience. Also, thank you for embarking with me on this knitter's voyage.

Stitch Bibliography

Parry-Jones, Maria
Knitting Stitch Bible, The
Page 39, Simple Eyelets
Page 194, Adapted to Merry Go Stripe

Stanfield, Lesley
New Knitting Stitch Library, The
Page 29, Basketweave

Starmore, Alice
Alice Starmore's Charts for Color Knitting
Page 60, Simple Argyle
Page 92, Croquet Wickets
Page 116, Adapted to Sweet Clover

Walker, Barbara G.
A Treasury of Knitting Patterns
Page 17, Tiny Texture
Page 205, Crest of the Wave
Page 255, Kisses and Hugs

A 2nd Treasury of Knitting Patterns
Page 266, Sparkling Lace

Charted Knitting Designs
Page 96, Windblown Cable

Resources

Berroco Inc.
1 Tupperware Drive
Suite 4
North Smithfield, RI 02896-6815
(401) 769-1212
www.berroco.com

JHB International Inc.
1955 S. Quince St.
Denver, CO 80231
(800) 525-9007
www.buttons.com

Westminster Fibers
(SMC)
165 Ledge St.
Nashua, NH 03060
(800) 445-9276
www.westminsterfibers.com

Plymouth Yarn Co.
500 Lafayette St.
Bristol, PA 19007
(215) 788-0459
www.plymouthyarn.com

Cascade Yarns
1224 Andover Park E.
Tukwila, WA 98188
(206) 574-0440
www.cascadeyarns.com